21-Day Cortisol Detox Plan for Women

Lose Weight, Sleep Better & Feel Like Yourself Again

GIALDA REED

Published by
GRAPEVINE BOOKS

www.grapevinebooks.com
email: contact@grapevinebooks.com

Ordering Information:
Quantity sales: Special discounts are available on quantity purchases by corporations, associations, and others.
For details, reach out to the publisher.

First published by Grapevine Books, 2025

CONTENTS

Introduction

How This **21**-Day Plan Helps You Lose Weight, Sleep Better & Reclaim Your Spark 8

Part I THE CORTISOL CODE Why You're Exhausted, Gaining Weight, and Waking Up at 3AM

What Is Cortisol and Why It Matters 10
Signs You're in Hormonal Survival Mode 14
Why "Eat Less, Move More" Doesn't Work 17
The Chain Reaction: Cravings, Weight Gain & **3** AM Wakeups 20
The **3** Biggest Mistakes Keeping Your Cortisol High 23
Sleep Repair: Fix **3**AM Wakeups, Cortisol Surges and Nighttime Anxiety 27
Feeling Like Yourself Again: Mood, Motivation and Hormone-Driven Confidence 31

PART II: THE 5-TRIGGER DETOX PROTOCOL

The CORE Method & **5**-Trigger Reset Explained 34
Nutritional Reset: What to Eat and When 37
Metabolic Timing for Real Results 40
Movement That Heals, Not Harms 44
Adaptogens & Supplements That Actually Work 50
Emotional Support and Cortisol-Friendly Mindset Shifts 53

PART III: YOUR 21-DAY CORTISOL DETOX PLAN

Emergency Fixes: What to Do When You Can't Sleep, Crave Sugar, or Feel Exhausted 63
After-Detox Reset for Lasting Weight Loss & Sleep Rhythm 66

PART IV: Detox-Friendly Recipes for Hormone Balance & Fat Burn

Sleep-Supporting Meals **70**

Fat-Burning Dinners **79**

Craving Crushers **82**

Cortisol-Calming Drinks **87**

PART V: Lifestyle Support & Printable Detox Tools

The Busy Woman's Guide to Cortisol-Friendly Meal Prepping **91**

Work-Life Balance Hacks to Lower Daily Stress **95**

21-Day Cortisol Detox Daily Workbook **100**

Cortisol Detox Daily Tracker & Reflection Journal **103**

INTRODUCTION

Welcome to the Cortisol Reset Journey

This isn't just another wellness book. It's not a plan to lose **10** pounds in **10** days, or a trendy detox that leaves you more tired than when you began. This is a recalibration—a reset for your body, your mind, and your rhythm of life. You didn't land here because you need another fix. You're here because something deeper within you knows it's time to feel differently. To feel whole again.

The Cortisol Reset Journey isn't about chasing a new version of yourself. It's about remembering the one you've always been, underneath the exhaustion, anxiety, and endless "shoulds." The woman who used to wake up with energy, laugh with ease, eat without guilt, and move through life with presence. She hasn't disappeared. She's just been buried beneath the weight of stress and survival.

Maybe you've spent years trying to "solve" yourself. You've read the books, tracked your macros, switched diets, signed up for challenges, and bought more supplements than you care to admit. But your energy still crashes. You still feel wired at night, foggy during the day, and heavier—in body and mind—than you used to.

That's not a failure. That's your body asking for something different. For rhythm, not restriction. For safety, not stimulation. For healing, not hacking.

This journey is about coming home to your body. It's about learning how cortisol—your body's stress hormone—has been both your protector and your limiter. When cortisol is balanced, you feel alert, clear, and stable. But when it's chronically elevated or depleted, your entire system—metabolism, mood, hormones, sleep—goes into disarray.

You're not here to "fix" yourself. You're here to realign. To understand the signals your body's been trying to send. And most importantly, to create a life that no longer demands constant survival mode.

Over the next few chapters, you'll learn why cortisol is the key to unlocking your health, your energy, and your peace. You'll understand how daily rhythms, not drastic overhauls, reset your internal systems. And you'll receive practical, compassionate tools to gently shift from burnout to balance.

This is not about intensity. It's about intentionality. Small, consistent choices. Trusting your body again. Restoring what stress has stolen.

So, take a deep breath. Unclench your jaw. Relax your shoulders. You've just taken the first real step not toward perfection—but toward peace.

Welcome to the Cortisol Reset Journey. Let's begin.

You're Not Broken — You're Burnt Out

Somewhere along the way, you were taught that if you just tried harder, you'd feel better. That if you stuck to the meal plan, pushed through your fatigue, hit the gym harder, drank more water, journaled your gratitude, and thought more positive thoughts... your body would cooperate. You'd have more energy. You'd sleep better. Your jeans would fit again. You'd feel like yourself again.

But the truth is, you've done all of that—and still, your body feels like it's betraying you. The scale won't budge. Your brain fog gets worse. Your sleep is shallow. You feel wired but tired, busy but unproductive, hungry but unsatisfied. The harder you try, the more it seems to backfire.

That doesn't mean you're broken.

It means you're burnt out.

Your body isn't malfunctioning—it's protecting you. The fatigue, the cravings, the weight gain, the insomnia—they're not signs of failure. They're signs of overload. Your body has been trying to keep you alive, to keep you safe, in a world that constantly tells it to push harder.

Burnout isn't just emotional exhaustion. It's a full-body shutdown that begins in the nervous system and spreads into every corner of your biology—your hormones, your metabolism, your immune system, your sleep cycles, even your digestion.

This is the cost of living in survival mode.

Survival Mode Looks Like Productivity

You might still be checking off your to-do list, managing your home, replying to messages, and performing well at work—but inside, you feel like you're unraveling. You're operating on borrowed energy, running on coffee and willpower, collapsing at night but unable to rest.

You put on makeup. You smile through meetings. You plan meals. You show up for everyone else. But something inside you whispers that this isn't sustainable. That you're stretched thin. That your fuse is shorter than it used to be. That your body is sending signals you don't know how to read anymore.

That quiet knowing is your wake-up call.

You're not imagining it. This isn't just "aging" or "modern life" or "mom brain." This is physiological burnout—the moment your body stops trying to keep up with the pressure and instead starts shutting down non-essential functions just to survive.

And cortisol is at the heart of it.

The Burnout-Cortisol Connection

When you face a stressful event, your body releases cortisol to help you respond. It's designed to be temporary. You escape the threat, your body calms, and hormone levels return to baseline.

But what happens when the threat never ends?

What happens when it's not a tiger chasing you, but a string of emails at midnight, unpaid bills, emotional stress, caretaking responsibilities, body shame, or unresolved trauma? Your body can't tell the difference. It just keeps producing cortisol to "save" you.

At first, cortisol keeps you going. It helps you feel focused, awake, and alert. But over time, this chronic release of cortisol starts to take a toll. Your blood sugar rises. Inflammation increases. Estrogen and progesterone get disrupted. Your thyroid slows down. Your gut weakens. Your sleep disappears. And eventually, the very hormone that was trying to help you becomes the reason you feel stuck.

This is why your energy crashes at **3** PM, your belly won't flatten, and your cravings spiral out of control. It's not because you need more discipline. It's because your body is desperately trying to keep you alive.

The Shame of "Not Getting It Together"

One of the cruelest tricks burnout plays is making you feel like it's your fault.

You look around and see other women who seem to be handling it all with ease. You start to wonder: What's wrong with me? Why can't I bounce back like I used to? Why does everything feel so hard now?

But you don't see their silent struggles, their night sweats, their racing thoughts, their hidden blood work, or the emotional labor they carry. Burnout thrives in silence. And cortisol dysfunction hides behind performance. Just because you're functioning doesn't mean you're okay.

High-achieving women are especially vulnerable to burnout because they've trained themselves to override every signal. To keep pushing when they're tired. To say yes when they need to say no. To put others first while ignoring their own needs. To live from the neck up and dismiss the body as something to be managed, controlled, or shamed into submission.

But your body isn't a machine.

It's not meant to operate under chronic stress and constant perfection. It's not designed to thrive in an environment of "not enough"—not enough rest, not enough nourishment, not enough joy, not enough safety.

The good news? You can retrain it. Not through punishment—but through rhythm, support, and compassion.

Your Body Isn't Fighting You. It's Fighting For You.

Every symptom you're experiencing is your body trying to communicate: I need something different.

That "extra" belly fat? It's cortisol protecting your organs.

That fatigue? It's your body begging for deep rest.

That irritability? It's your nervous system on edge.

That anxiety? It's your brain anticipating the next threat.

That sugar craving? It's a cry for quick energy and comfort.

Once you stop fighting these signals—and start listening to them—you'll discover they were never working against you. They were trying to keep you alive.

And now, you get to tell your body: We're safe. It's okay to heal now.

You don't need to fix yourself. You need to create the right environment for your body to stop defending and start repairing. That begins with regulating cortisol—not by suppressing it, but by teaching your body how to feel safe again.

That's what this book will show you how to do.

It's not a fix. It's a reset. A return to rhythm. A reconnection with your body's natural intelligence. A gentle invitation to trust your biology again.

You're not broken.

You're burnt out.

But that ends now.

How This 21-Day Plan Helps You Lose Weight, Sleep Better & Reclaim Your Spark

Welcome to a new approach. One that does not shame you into cutting calories or push you through punishing workouts. Instead, it works with your body to reset what is truly out of balance: your cortisol. This **21**-day plan is built around three key pillars that directly target the root causes of weight gain, sleep disruption, and that feeling of exhaustion where you no longer recognize yourself.

Let's break it down.

1. Fat Loss Without Starvation

You have likely heard the old advice: eat less, move more. But if that has failed to deliver results, there is a reason. When your cortisol levels are dysregulated, your body enters survival mode. It stores fat, especially around the belly, slows metabolism, and becomes resistant to weight loss. This plan is not about restriction. It is about lowering cortisol through the right foods, smart meal timing, and gentle movement that heals instead of harms.

In these **21** days, you will focus on nourishing whole foods that stabilize blood sugar, reduce inflammation, and support your hormone balance. You will eat enough to feel satisfied and energized. This is not a diet. It is a metabolic reset. When your body feels safe, it naturally lets go of excess fat. And that starts with calming your internal stress signals, not starving yourself.

2. Sleep Repair That Starts During the Day

If you find yourself wide awake at **3** AM or dragging through the afternoon even after a full night's rest, it is not just poor sleep habits. It is likely your cortisol rhythm that needs repair. Cortisol is meant to rise in the morning and fall at night. But stress, poor nutrition, and erratic routines can flip this rhythm upside down.

This plan is designed to restore that natural rise-and-fall pattern. Through small but powerful habits like morning sunlight exposure, calming nutrients, and a steady wind-down routine, you will gradually reset your internal clock. The food you eat during the day, the timing of your meals, and even your breathwork practices will all support deeper, more consistent sleep.

Most women report improved sleep within the first two weeks. Fewer wakeups. More energy upon rising. Better sleep also boosts fat loss, emotional stability, and overall vitality.

3. Energy and Mood Reset: Feel Like Yourself Again

That drained, foggy feeling is not a personal failure. It is a signal. Chronic high cortisol can steal nutrients, spike anxiety, and leave you disconnected from your own energy and emotions. You may feel flat, irritable, or numb without really knowing why.

This plan rebuilds your energy system layer by layer. You will learn nervous system reset tools like breathing and grounding, incorporate mood-stabilizing foods, and gently reintroduce motivation through small wins. You will also explore adaptogens that support the adrenal system and learn to reframe the perfectionism and pressure that keep your body stuck in overdrive.

You will begin to recognize yourself again. Not just in the mirror, but in the way you laugh, move, think, and feel.

This Is More Than a Detox

This plan is not a temporary fix or a quick cleanse. It is a **21**-day structured reset built for women who are tired of doing everything right but getting nowhere. It is for those who want to stop guessing and start healing.

By the end of this plan, you can expect to:

- Lose weight without feeling hungry
- Sleep deeper and longer
- Wake up with more natural energy
- Think more clearly and feel emotionally lighter
- Reconnect with the vibrant, powerful version of yourself

The spark is still there. This plan will help you find it again, day by day. Let's begin.

PART I THE CORTISOL CODE WHY YOU'RE EXHAUSTED, GAINING WEIGHT, AND WAKING UP AT 3AM

What Is Cortisol and Why It Matters

It starts like this: your alarm goes off at **6:30** AM. You hit snooze twice, already feeling a weight in your limbs. You drag yourself out of bed, eyes gritty, head foggy. You haven't even started the day, but you feel like you've run a marathon. You shuffle to the kitchen, pour the coffee before you even open your eyes fully, and hope it kicks in fast. You get through the morning with caffeine and grit, powering through tasks, school drop-offs, emails, appointments. By **3** PM, you crash. Hard. You crave sugar, salt, something to keep you upright. You push through, again. At night, you're so tired you can't think, but when you finally get to bed, your mind won't shut off. You stare at the ceiling, wide awake at **2:47** AM.

This isn't laziness. It's not lack of motivation. It's cortisol.

Cortisol is one of the most misunderstood hormones in your body. Often dubbed the "stress hormone," it's actually a critical part of your day-to-day survival. Produced by your adrenal glands, cortisol regulates energy, blood sugar, blood pressure, immune response, inflammation, and metabolism. It's also responsible for your body's fight-or-flight response. You need it. You just don't need it all the time.

The Natural Cortisol Curve

In a healthy body, cortisol follows a rhythm. It rises in the early morning to wake you up and help you feel alert. It peaks between **7–9** AM, then slowly tapers off throughout the day, reaching its lowest point at bedtime. This cycle is what keeps you energized in the morning, focused in the afternoon, and ready for rest at night.

That's the ideal curve. But in today's high-pressure world, very few people are actually living with this healthy cortisol rhythm. Instead, we're dealing with either chronically elevated cortisol—where you feel wired, anxious, and can't sleep—or flattened cortisol—where you feel tired all day and struggle to function.

When that natural curve breaks down, the body stops knowing what time it is, literally. Your internal clock, or circadian rhythm, gets out of sync. You may feel wide awake late at night, groggy in the morning, and struggle with irregular energy throughout the day.

Cortisol's Job in the Body

Cortisol is released in response to stress, and stress can be physical, emotional, or environmental. It doesn't matter if you're escaping a burning building or scrolling your phone at midnight reading bad news—your brain perceives stress the same way.

When cortisol is released in short bursts, it helps you survive. It gives you energy, sharpens your focus, and temporarily suppresses functions that aren't essential in a crisis—like digestion or reproduction. In that way, cortisol is incredibly helpful.

But problems arise when the stress never ends.

Because cortisol affects so many systems, chronic overproduction can wreak havoc in unexpected ways. High cortisol leads to:

- Increased abdominal fat
- Blood sugar instability
- Mood swings and irritability
- Weakened immunity
- Digestive problems
- Disrupted sleep cycles
- Irregular or painful periods

- Fatigue and low motivation
- Brain fog and poor memory

If your body is producing too much cortisol for too long, it begins to wear down your resilience. It moves from helping you survive to keeping you stuck.

Why Most People Don't Realize It's Cortisol

Cortisol dysfunction doesn't feel like a crisis at first. It feels like subtle shifts in how you function. You start reaching for caffeine more often. Your sleep becomes lighter, but you ignore it. You feel foggy, but chalk it up to age or stress. You get bloated or crave more sugar and think it's just bad eating. You don't connect the dots.

That's because cortisol doesn't act in isolation. It affects almost every other hormone in your body, especially insulin, estrogen, progesterone, and thyroid hormones. So instead of one clear symptom, you get dozens of small ones. And most of them are dismissed, normalized, or misdiagnosed.

You may go to your doctor with complaints of fatigue, weight gain, or insomnia and be told it's just stress. Or worse, that it's all in your head. But if cortisol is at the root, no amount of willpower or temporary fixes will work. You can't out-discipline a misfiring hormone.

When Cortisol Gets Stuck

There are three common patterns when cortisol becomes dysregulated:

1. High All Day

You feel on edge all the time. You can't relax. Your heart races with minor stress. You're easily overwhelmed. You may feel wired at night but exhausted in the morning. Sleep is broken or hard to come by. This is early-stage cortisol dysregulation—your body is pumping it out constantly.

2. High at the Wrong Times

Your cortisol levels might be too low in the morning (you can't get out of bed) and spike late at night (you can't sleep). You might feel tired and wired at the same time. This pattern disrupts your circadian rhythm and makes energy management nearly impossible.

3. Flatlined

After years of overproduction, your adrenal system may crash. Cortisol output flattens. You feel numb, heavy, and detached. Even small tasks feel monumental. This isn't laziness or depression. It's exhaustion at a cellular level.

Understanding your cortisol pattern is key to choosing the right strategies for healing. What works for someone with high cortisol might be completely wrong for someone with a flatline pattern.

Not Just a Stress Problem—a Lifestyle Loop

Most cortisol imbalances aren't caused by one big trauma. They come from dozens of small stressors repeated every day:

- Skipping meals
- Overtraining

- Poor sleep
- Inflammatory foods
- Emotional suppression
- Financial stress
- Caffeine dependence
- Over-scheduling
- Lack of sunlight and movement

The body adds these up. It doesn't differentiate between emotional and physical stress. It just reacts.

The problem isn't just the stress itself—it's the lack of recovery. Cortisol only becomes a threat when it doesn't turn off. But the good news is, the same hormone that keeps you stuck in survival mode can also be rebalanced. You don't need to eliminate all stress. You need to restore the rhythm of stress and recovery.

Why This Matters for Women

Cortisol affects women differently. It interferes with estrogen, progesterone, and thyroid hormones—making it harder to lose weight, regulate mood, or maintain a healthy menstrual cycle. It also affects women's ability to sleep, digest, and recover.

Women are also more likely to override their symptoms. We're taught to be productive, selfless, and emotionally composed. So when fatigue or anxiety shows up, we push through. We don't slow down until our body forces us to.

That's why cortisol balance is not just a medical issue—it's a cultural one. Learning to regulate cortisol is about reclaiming your right to rest, nourish, move gently, and feel.

When you understand cortisol, you stop blaming yourself for being tired, overwhelmed, or foggy. You realize your body has been doing its best under impossible conditions. And that means healing is not only possible—it's expected.

You just have to give your body a different set of signals. And that journey starts now.

Signs You're in Hormonal Survival Mode

When your body is stuck in hormonal survival mode, it doesn't always scream. It whispers. It sends subtle signals, physical and emotional, that something is off. Most of us miss these signs because we've normalized exhaustion, irritability, and disconnection. But when these signals go unaddressed, they become chronic—and they quietly drain your health.

Survival mode is not a personality trait or mental weakness. It's a biological state where your body prioritizes safety above all else. Your stress system (mainly cortisol) dominates, and in the process, other systems—reproductive, digestive, cognitive—get downgraded. You feel off, but you can't always explain why.

Below is a practical checklist to help you assess whether your body is stuck in hormonal survival mode.

Cortisol Survival Mode Checklist

Check all that apply to you:

ENERGY & FATIGUE

☐ I wake up feeling tired, even after a full night's sleep

☐ I rely on caffeine or sugar to "get going"

☐ I crash in the afternoon and feel unproductive

☐ I feel tired but wired in the evening

☐ I feel exhausted all the time but can't nap or rest

SLEEP

☐ I struggle to fall asleep at night

☐ I wake up in the middle of the night and can't fall back asleep

☐ I often wake between **2–4** AM

☐ I never feel fully rested, no matter how long I sleep

☐ My dreams are intense, vivid, or disturbing

MOOD & MENTAL HEALTH

❑ I feel anxious or overwhelmed by simple things

❑ I get irritable or short-tempered easily

❑ I feel numb, detached, or emotionally flat

❑ I have difficulty focusing or remembering things

❑ I often feel like I'm on edge, even when nothing is wrong

WEIGHT & METABOLISM

❑ I have gained weight (especially around my midsection)

❑ My weight won't budge no matter what I eat or how much I exercise

❑ I feel bloated or inflamed most of the time

❑ My hunger feels erratic—I either forget to eat or can't stop snacking

❑ I crave carbs or sugar daily, especially at night

DIGESTION

❑ I feel bloated after eating, even small meals

❑ I experience gas, constipation, or irregular bowel movements

❑ My digestion feels sluggish or unpredictable

❑ I often feel heavy or slow after meals

❑ I have food sensitivities that seem to be increasing

HORMONES & REPRODUCTIVE HEALTH

❑ My periods are irregular, painful, or have changed significantly

❑ I experience intense PMS, mood swings, or breast tenderness

❑ My libido has decreased or disappeared

❑ I have PCOS, thyroid issues, or endometriosis

❑ I feel like my hormones are "out of control"

OTHER PHYSICAL SIGNS

❑ My hair is thinning or falling out more than usual

❑ My skin feels dry, dull, or more reactive

❑ My hands or feet are often cold

❑ I bruise easily or heal slowly

❑ I feel dizzy or lightheaded when I stand up too fast

Interpretation:

- If you checked **5–10** boxes, you may be entering hormonal survival mode
- If you checked **11–20** boxes, you are likely operating in chronic stress mode
- If you checked **21**+ boxes, your body is likely in full hormonal burnout

This isn't a diagnosis. It's a mirror. Your body is communicating. These signs are not failures but feedback.

Exercise: Hormone Story Mapping Reflection

Fill this out to better understand your body's patterns and needs

1. My energy feels highest around:

2. My energy crashes hardest at:

3. I usually crave (food/drink/emotion):

4. The last time I truly felt "balanced" or well in my body was:

5. The three most noticeable changes in my body over the past year have been:

-
-
-

6. The signs I've been ignoring or minimizing include:

7. If my body could speak right now, it would say:

8. One gentle shift I'm ready to make this week is:

This exercise is a reset in itself. By slowing down to reflect, you're already stepping out of reactivity and into regulation. Awareness is the first phase of healing. Before the supplements, before the meal plans, before the routines—comes listening.

You are not being dramatic. You are not imagining things. Your body is wise, and it's asking for attention, not perfection. The next chapters will give you the tools to respond—gently, effectively, and in rhythm with the biology that has always been on your side.

Why "Eat Less, Move More" Doesn't Work

You decide to finally get serious. No more excuses. Monday starts the new routine. You cut your calories, wake up early to squeeze in a **45**-minute workout, and swap lunch with a salad. By day three, you're already tired, irritable, and hungry. You push through anyway. By day seven, you're exhausted, still not seeing results, and craving sugar like your life depends on it. You snap at your kids, cancel your workout, and raid the pantry at **9** PM. You wonder, "What is wrong with me? Why can't I stick to this?"

The answer? Because your body isn't being stubborn. It's being smart.

The idea that all bodies will respond to "eat less, move more" is not only outdated—it's actively harmful to women living with cortisol dysregulation and hormonal imbalance. It assumes the body is a simple math equation. But your biology is far more complex than calories in, calories out.

The Oversimplified Formula

"Eat less, move more" was built on the notion that weight loss is purely a matter of discipline. If you want to lose fat, just burn more than you consume. It's a tempting idea. Simple. Linear. Easy to package and sell.

But the female body, particularly under stress, does not follow this formula. Hormones play a massive role in how you burn, store, and respond to food and movement. And when cortisol is out of balance, the rules of the game change completely.

Let's break it down.

Why Eating Less Backfires Under Stress

Your body is hardwired for survival. When food intake drops significantly—especially while cortisol is elevated—it interprets that as a threat. Starvation mode kicks in. Instead of burning fat, your body starts conserving it.

Here's what actually happens:

- Cortisol increases further in response to restriction
- Thyroid function slows to preserve energy
- Muscle mass is broken down for fuel, reducing your metabolic rate
- Fat storage increases, especially in the abdomen
- Cravings intensify as the body demands quick energy
- Sleep becomes disrupted, which further affects weight and hunger hormones

You might lose a few pounds initially, but your body is working behind the scenes to protect itself. That protection often looks like a plateau... or even weight gain.

Now combine that with mental stress, under-eating, and poor sleep, and your body enters a full defensive state. It doesn't care about fitting into your jeans. It cares about surviving a perceived famine.

Why More Exercise Doesn't Always Help

Exercise is good. But like anything, too much—or the wrong type—at the wrong time can work against you.

For women with high cortisol or adrenal fatigue, intense exercise (like long runs, HIIT, or boot camps) can do more harm than good. These workouts raise cortisol even further, placing more stress on an already overwhelmed system.

What this might look like:

- You work out five times a week, but you're constantly tired
- You feel bloated or inflamed post-workout
- You don't sleep well after an intense gym day
- You feel hungrier and moodier, not calmer or stronger
- Your body holds onto weight, especially around your belly

When your system is in a chronic stress loop, exercise needs to be a signal of safety, not punishment. Restorative movement—like walking, yoga, gentle strength training, or stretching—can lower cortisol and support fat loss more effectively in this state.

You don't need to train harder. You need to train smarter, in alignment with your current physiology.

The Hidden Cost of Forcing Results

Here's what no one talks about: the emotional damage done by following a plan that works against your body. You start internalizing the failure. You tell yourself you're not trying hard enough. You compare yourself to others. You start to believe that something is wrong with you.

But your body has been responding appropriately to stress the whole time.

"Eat less, move more" doesn't take into account:

- Blood sugar fluctuations
- Cortisol spikes and dips
- Estrogen-progesterone imbalances
- Sleep deprivation
- Inflammation
- Trauma and emotional suppression
- Digestive issues
- Nervous system overload

It treats your body like a calculator, not a conversation.

So What Actually Works?

When you reset your cortisol rhythm, everything changes. Your hunger cues begin to stabilize. Your cravings decrease. Your sleep deepens. Your metabolism regulates naturally. Fat loss becomes a side effect of healing—not the goal.

Instead of pushing harder, you learn to listen closer.

Instead of cutting food, you learn when and what to eat to support hormonal balance.

Instead of punishing workouts, you adopt movement that helps your body feel safe and strong again.

Instead of shame, you build trust.

The path out of survival mode isn't paved with more restriction and output. It's built on nourishment, rhythm, and respect for the systems that have kept you going, even when life was asking too much.

Your Body Has Always Been On Your Side

If "eat less, move more" has failed you, it's not because you failed. It's because that model wasn't built for a body under chronic stress. Your biology is intelligent. It resists being starved and overworked because it wants to protect you.

And now, with the right signals, it will begin to release the tension, the weight, the fatigue, the inflammation. Not because you've forced it to, but because you've shown it something new.

Safety.

The rest of this reset is about doing just that. Teaching your body it is no longer in danger. That it is safe to heal. Safe to rest. Safe to let go.

The Chain Reaction: Cravings, Weight Gain & 3 AM Wakeups

It often starts with something small. You stay up too late one night. You skip breakfast the next morning. You power through work, too busy to eat properly. By mid-afternoon, you're ravenous. You grab something sugary, salty, or quick. You feel slightly better—until the crash. Then come the cravings. The irritability. The brain fog. The bloating. You push through the evening with more snacks or another coffee, and when you finally get to bed, your body refuses to settle. At exactly **3:07** AM, you're wide awake. Alert. Anxious. Wired.

This isn't just poor planning. It's a hormonal chain reaction. And it's fueled by cortisol.

Cortisol doesn't just control your stress response. It interacts with virtually every system in your body—especially your blood sugar, appetite, and sleep patterns. When cortisol is off, everything is off. Cravings become intense. Fat becomes harder to lose. Sleep becomes fragmented. And unfortunately, the more you try to "fix" one part—like controlling cravings—the more the others often get worse.

It Begins with Blood Sugar

When cortisol is elevated, your liver releases stored glucose into the bloodstream so your body has quick energy to deal with a "threat." If there's no real danger (just stress), that glucose still floods your system. Your pancreas then pumps out insulin to bring sugar levels down. But with cortisol still in the mix, the balance never stabilizes.

You swing from high blood sugar to low blood sugar—repeatedly.

Low blood sugar triggers hunger, irritability, and cravings. Your body begins to crave the fastest energy source it knows: sugar and refined carbs. Not because you're weak—but because your blood sugar rollercoaster is demanding fuel.

Cortisol and Cravings

Many women blame themselves for their cravings. But in truth, cortisol has a powerful impact on your appetite. High cortisol increases a hormone called ghrelin (your hunger hormone) and suppresses leptin (your fullness hormone). So you feel hungrier, even after eating. And the food you crave is more likely to be processed, high in sugar or salt, and less nutrient-dense.

Even emotional cravings can be hormonally rooted. When cortisol is high and serotonin is low, your body will seek out foods that quickly boost pleasure chemicals—like chocolate, chips, or bread.

You may eat, but still not feel satisfied. That's not because you lack control. It's because your body is asking for stability, not just calories.

How Belly Fat Builds—And Why It's So Stubborn

Cortisol's job is to keep you alive—not to help you lose weight. When your body perceives any kind of ongoing stress (physical, emotional, dietary, or even mental pressure), it enters conservation mode. That means storing energy rather than burning it. And when it comes to storing fat, cortisol has a favorite spot: your belly.

This isn't random. Belly fat—technically called visceral fat—is metabolically active. It sits deep within the abdominal cavity, surrounding your internal organs. Unlike subcutaneous fat (which lies just under the skin), visceral fat is highly responsive to cortisol. It's your body's way of protecting vital organs during perceived danger. But in modern life, the "danger" is chronic stress, and that protection becomes harmful.

High cortisol levels trigger your body to divert calories into fat storage, especially around the midsection. It's a survival reflex rooted in evolution. The body assumes famine or danger is coming and prepares by holding onto fat in the most protective location. This fat isn't inert—it releases its own stress signals, creating a hormonal echo chamber. The more cortisol you produce, the more belly fat you store. And the more belly fat you have, the more inflammatory signals your body generates, keeping cortisol high.

This feedback loop is one reason belly fat is so stubborn. Even when you're eating clean or working out, your body might still resist letting it go—because it sees that fat as necessary for survival. It doesn't know you're following a wellness program. It only knows whether it feels safe.

There's another hidden factor too: insulin resistance. When cortisol spikes repeatedly due to stress, it also causes repeated spikes in blood sugar. Over time, this dulls your cells' sensitivity to insulin—the hormone that moves sugar out of the bloodstream and into your cells. When insulin isn't working properly, your body stores more fat and struggles to burn it efficiently. This worsens abdominal weight gain, often even in women who are eating nutrient-dense meals and working out regularly.

The result? You feel like your body is betraying you. You're doing "everything right" but nothing changes. The truth is, your body isn't defying you. It's trying to protect you. The excess fat is a response to a stress environment—internal or external. Until you create safety and lower cortisol, your body has no reason to release that stored energy.

The solution is not to slash calories, cut carbs, or add harder workouts. In fact, those approaches often make it worse. The solution is to stabilize blood sugar, calm the nervous system, and shift out of survival mode. When your body feels nourished and secure, it will stop clinging to belly fat. It will begin to let go, gently, in its own time—not through force, but through rhythm.

This expanded version provides deeper insight into the why, how, and what to do about it—matching the tone and structure of the chapter while reinforcing your subtitle promise to "burn belly fat."

The Mystery of the 3 AM Wakeup

Waking up around **3** AM isn't random. It's a biological response to stress hormones peaking at the wrong time. Your cortisol should be low at night. But when your system is dysregulated, it may spike in the middle of the night—especially if your blood sugar crashes while you're sleeping.

Low blood sugar is a stress event for the body. Cortisol rises to help stabilize it. But that surge also wakes you up.

You may notice a racing heart, mental alertness, or an anxious feeling. You're not dreaming. You're dealing with cortisol in real time.

Over time, this broken sleep leads to even higher cortisol levels the next day, more cravings, more stress, and less metabolic function. The chain reaction deepens.

Breaking the Cycle

You can't break the chain by tackling symptoms in isolation. Instead, you must restore rhythm. Here's what helps:

- Eat regular, balanced meals that include protein, fat, and slow carbs
- Never skip breakfast—especially if you're under stress
- Avoid extreme fasting or very low-carb diets until cortisol stabilizes
- Use food to anchor your blood sugar before bed (e.g., a protein snack)
- Cut back on caffeine, especially in the afternoon
- Prioritize rest over intense workouts during high-stress periods
- Use calming practices before bed (breathing, stretching, reading)

You don't need to force discipline. You need to create safety. Once your body feels stable, it will stop clinging to fat, chasing sugar, and waking you up at night. It's not willpower—it's chemistry.

My Chain Reaction Journal

Use this space to track the subtle ways your body may be stuck in the cortisol-cravings-weight-sleep loop. Fill it out honestly—this isn't about judgment. It's about awareness.

1. What time of day do I usually crave sugar or carbs?

2. What do I typically eat (or skip) before those cravings hit?

3. When was the last time I woke up in the middle of the night? What time was it?

4. What did I eat for dinner or as a bedtime snack that night?

5. What emotion or sensation do I usually feel when cravings hit?

☐ *Tired*

☐ *Anxious*

☐ *Bored*

☐ *Sad*

☐ *Restless*

☐ *Other: ___________*

6. What does my body really need in those moments (beyond food)?

7. One small change I can try this week to balance my rhythm is:

Every time you map this out, you give your body a new chance to feel supported instead of starved. Cravings and wakeups are not random. They're part of a loop. And now, you're learning how to interrupt it—with rhythm, not restriction.

The 3 Biggest Mistakes Keeping Your Cortisol High

You've tried the supplements. You've cleaned up your diet. You've committed to better sleep. And still, your energy crashes, your belly won't budge, and your brain feels like it's been dipped in fog. If you've been doing "all the right things" and not feeling better, it's time to look at the habits and hidden beliefs that may be unknowingly keeping your cortisol elevated.

Cortisol isn't the enemy. You need it to wake up, focus, and manage stress. But when it stays high too often for too long, it disrupts almost every system in your body. The goal isn't to eliminate cortisol—it's to restore its rhythm. That means reducing the daily patterns that tell your body it's not safe.

Let's break down the three most common mistakes women make—often with the best intentions—that keep cortisol levels high and hormones out of balance.

Mistake #1: Skipping Meals (Especially Breakfast)

You may think you're giving your body a break by skipping breakfast or pushing your first meal to noon. Maybe you're following intermittent fasting trends, or maybe mornings are just too chaotic. But if you're in hormonal survival mode, skipping meals is one of the fastest ways to spike cortisol.

When you go too long without food, your blood sugar drops. This signals a stress response, and cortisol is released to raise your blood sugar back up. In a body that's already stressed, this response only intensifies fatigue, cravings, and brain fog. Over time, it leads to unstable energy, emotional eating, and disrupted sleep.

Skipping breakfast is especially damaging. Cortisol is meant to be highest in the morning, and eating within the first hour of waking helps bring it down naturally. Without that early nourishment, your body stays in a "stress alert" state all day.

Instead:

Eat a balanced breakfast with protein, fat, and slow-digesting carbs within **60** minutes of waking. Avoid sugary cereals or coffee on an empty stomach. Think eggs with avocado and sweet potato, or oats with chia seeds and nut butter.

Mistake #2: Pushing Through Exhaustion

You know that voice in your head—the one that says, "Just get it done"? The one that tells you to finish the emails, clean the kitchen, go to that class, keep hustling? That voice may be motivating, but if your body is already depleted, it's also raising your cortisol every time you ignore the need for rest.

Pushing through exhaustion sends a powerful signal to your nervous system: we're not safe to slow down. And that message keeps cortisol pumping. The more you override your body's cues, the more you stay locked in stress mode. You don't have to be anxious or panicking to be flooded with stress hormones. Chronic productivity pressure is enough.

When you push without pause, your body starts cutting corners elsewhere. Digestion slows. Sleep gets lighter. Hormones fall out of rhythm. It's not that you're too busy to rest—it's that you've forgotten rest is productive.

Instead:

Start honoring your energy, not just your schedule. Build in micro-rests throughout the day. Sit down when you eat. Pause between tasks. Take five slow breaths when you transition between work and home. Give your body a few quiet moments where it doesn't have to be alert or reactive.

Mistake #3: Overdoing Exercise

Exercise is vital for mental health, metabolic balance, and longevity. But for a woman in burnout or survival mode, more movement isn't always better. In fact, overexercising—especially high-intensity or long-duration cardio—can keep cortisol stuck on high.

Your body perceives intense exercise as a form of stress. When you're already depleted, that extra push can feel like another threat to your system. Instead of helping you burn fat, it drives inflammation, increases hunger, and interferes with recovery.

You might feel worse after your workouts: tired, bloated, sore for days, mentally foggy. You may also start craving sugar or carbs more frequently after workouts. These are all signs your cortisol was spiked instead of soothed.

Instead:

Choose movement that sends a signal of safety. Walking, strength training, Pilates, mobility work, stretching, and low-impact cardio can be far more effective for regulating cortisol than punishing boot camps. The key isn't intensity—it's consistency and recovery.

What These Mistakes Have in Common

All three mistakes—skipping meals, ignoring rest, and overexercising—come from the same place: a culture that equates health with control. We've been taught that eating less, doing more, and pushing through discomfort are signs of strength.

But your body thrives in rhythm, not restriction. In nourishment, not urgency. In safety, not struggle.

High cortisol is not just about what you're doing. It's about what your body believes it needs to survive. These three mistakes, when repeated daily, convince your biology that you are under threat.

The reset begins when you stop reinforcing that belief.

Worksheet: Uncovering Your Hidden Cortisol Triggers

1. How often do you skip or delay breakfast?

☐ Rarely or never

☐ A few times a week

☐ Most days

What usually gets in the way of eating in the morning?

2. On a scale of 1 to 10, how often do you "push through" when your body feels tired?

(1 = never, 10 = constantly)

Rating: ______

What tasks or habits usually override your rest signals?

3. How does your current exercise routine make you feel afterward?

☐ Energized and calm

☐ Exhausted or shaky

☐ Sore for days

☐ Anxious or hungry

What type of movement actually feels good in your body right now?

4. Which of these supportive shifts are you open to trying this week?

☐ Eating breakfast within 60 minutes of waking

☐ Swapping one intense workout for a walk or stretch

☐ Taking a 10-minute rest without your phone

☐ Pausing before pushing through exhaustion

5. What is one small action I can take today to lower my cortisol?

These small changes are the beginning of hormonal recovery. You don't need a complete overhaul to feel better. You just need to stop sending your body the signal that it's unsafe. And that begins by removing the silent stressors—one rhythm at a time.

Sleep Repair: Fix 3AM Wakeups, Cortisol Surges and Nighttime Anxiety

You wake up groggy, even after a full night's sleep. You move through the day in a daze, using coffee or sugar to get through the afternoon. By evening, you're drained—but strangely alert when it's time to wind down. You scroll on your phone, can't fall asleep, and lie awake thinking about everything you didn't do. And then, the next morning, it starts all over again.

This is not just burnout. This is a biological loop. A hormonal feedback cycle. A full-body rhythm that's stuck in survival mode. And once your system is caught in it, everything starts to feel harder—thinking clearly, feeling motivated, managing your weight, and especially staying awake and energized.

For many women, sleep is the first thing to go when cortisol runs high. You may lie awake for hours even when you are exhausted. Or perhaps you fall asleep easily, only to wake up at **3** AM with your heart racing and mind spinning. Maybe you wake up groggy no matter how long you stay in bed. These are not random sleep problems. They are signs that your cortisol rhythm is out of balance. And until that rhythm is repaired, no amount of melatonin, white noise, or herbal tea will fix it.

In this chapter, we will dive into what is really going on, and how to gently restore a natural sleep rhythm that supports deep, nourishing rest. When you sleep well, everything else improves—your metabolism, your mood, your ability to lose weight and think clearly. Sleep is not just a symptom. It is a central part of healing.

Understanding the Cortisol-Sleep Connection

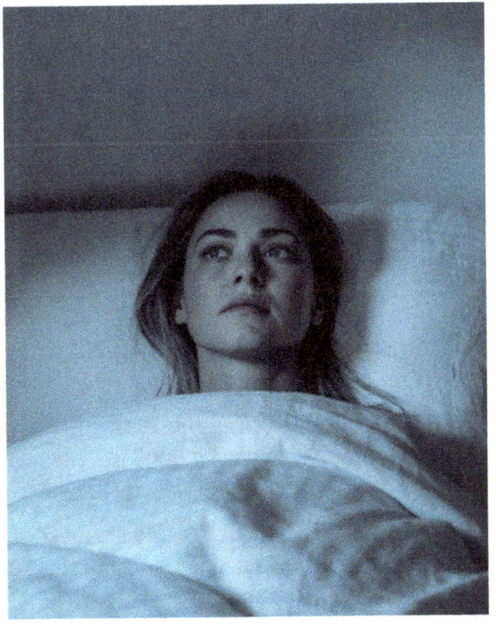

Cortisol is a hormone with a rhythm. It is supposed to rise in the morning to wake you up, peak a few hours after, and slowly taper off throughout the day so melatonin can take over at night. But when your body is stuck in fight-or-flight mode, that rhythm gets scrambled. Cortisol may stay high in the evening, making it hard to fall asleep. Or it may spike in the early morning hours, jolting you awake around **3** or **4** AM.

This can happen for many reasons: blood sugar crashes, inflammation, emotional stress, nutrient depletion, or even hidden sources of light or stimulation. The good news is that these patterns are not permanent. With the right support, your body can relearn how to sleep deeply and wake up naturally.

Why 3AM Wakeups Happen

If you regularly wake up in the middle of the night and feel alert or anxious, that is often a cortisol surge triggered by low blood sugar or stress hormones. During the night, your body shifts into repair mode. But if your system believes it is under threat—whether from a real danger or chronic emotional stress—it releases cortisol to "wake you up" and handle the threat.

Even minor triggers can set this off: eating too little at dinner, scrolling on your phone late into the night, skipping meals earlier in the day, or having a tense conversation before bed. The body is trying to protect you. But in doing so, it disrupts the one thing you need most—rest.

How This Plan Repairs Your Sleep

This **21**-day plan is designed to restore your cortisol rhythm step by step. Here is how.

1. Stabilizing Blood Sugar

Cortisol and blood sugar are deeply connected. When your blood sugar drops too low at night, cortisol steps in to bring it back up. This is why a light, protein-rich snack before bed can actually improve sleep. During this plan, your meals are structured to avoid sugar crashes. You will eat enough protein, healthy fat, and slow-burning carbs during the day to avoid the dips that cause nighttime wakeups.

2. Resetting the Rhythm with Light and Darkness

Your brain reads light as daytime and darkness as nighttime. This seems obvious, but in a world full of screens, artificial lighting, and late-night work habits, your natural rhythm can get confused. During this plan, you will be encouraged to get early morning sunlight exposure—ideally within the first hour of waking—and to reduce blue light exposure in the evening.

This simple habit tells your brain when to produce cortisol and when to let melatonin take over. It is one of the most powerful tools for resetting your sleep-wake cycle.

3. Calming the Nervous System at Night

The more your body feels safe, the less cortisol it needs to produce. This is especially important before bedtime. Instead of working or scrolling right up until you sleep, you will create a calming evening routine. This can include gentle stretching, a warm bath, reading a physical book, or practicing slow, deep breathing.

One of the simplest practices is the **4-7-8** breath: inhale for **4** seconds, hold for **7**, and exhale for **8**. Doing this for just a few minutes before bed helps shift your nervous system into a calm, restful state.

4. Supporting Sleep with Key Nutrients

Sleep is also influenced by what you eat. Magnesium, potassium, B vitamins, and amino acids all play a role in calming the brain and lowering cortisol. During this plan, you will eat more foods rich in these nutrients—like leafy greens, avocados, seeds, fatty fish, and turkey.

In some cases, a simple magnesium supplement in the evening can help the body relax more fully. Herbal teas like chamomile or lemon balm can also support rest without dependence.

5. Creating a Sleep-Safe Environment

Your bedroom should feel like a sanctuary. That means cool temperatures, no harsh lighting, and as little noise as possible. If you live in a noisy area, white noise or earplugs may help. If light creeps in, consider blackout curtains or a sleep mask. Even small improvements in your sleep environment can support cortisol regulation over time.

6. Releasing the Pressure to "Sleep Perfectly"

Lastly, be kind to yourself. Fixing sleep takes time. Some nights will be better than others. But as you follow this plan, your system will slowly shift. Try not to obsess over your sleep tracker or beat yourself up for waking up during the night. Progress is not linear, but it is real. Trust the process.

What to Expect Over the 21 Days

By the end of the first week, many women report falling asleep faster. By week two, they begin sleeping through the night more consistently. And by week three, they often wake up with more energy—without needing three cups of coffee.

Sleep is foundational to healing. When your body feels safe, rested, and restored, it can finally do what it is designed to do—release fat, calm inflammation, rebuild energy, and bring you back to life.

Sleep is not just rest. It is repair. And starting now, your repair has already begun.

Exercise: Mapping Your Survival Mode Cycle

1. How do your mornings typically feel?

☐ Energized and focused

☐ Foggy and slow

☐ Anxious or rushed

2. What time of day do you feel the biggest crash in energy?

☐ Late morning

☐ Afternoon

☐ Early evening

3. What do you reach for when you're tired or craving something?

☐ Sugar

☐ Caffeine

☐ Processed snacks

☐ Nothing—I just push through

4. When was the last time you felt truly rested after sleep?

5. How does your body usually respond to stress?

☐ I get wired and tense

☐ I shut down and get numb

☐ I lose focus or become irritable

6. What is one habit I use to push through when tired?

7. What is one rhythm I can try this week to support my energy naturally?

☐ Eat within an hour of waking

☐ Walk instead of a high-intensity workout

☐ Reduce screen time before bed

☐ Add a **10**-minute rest break mid-day

This is not a flaw in your motivation. It's a signal from your biology. Your body doesn't need punishment. It needs rhythm. And once that rhythm is restored, your energy will return—not in a burst, but in a steady, sustainable way.

Feeling Like Yourself Again: Mood, Motivation and Hormone-Driven Confidence

When was the last time you truly felt like yourself? Not just functioning or getting through the day, but feeling steady, confident, and joyful in your own skin? For many women dealing with high cortisol, that version of themselves feels like a distant memory. The one who had energy, laughed easily, got excited about plans, felt emotionally balanced, and didn't second-guess every decision. If you've been wondering where that woman went, this chapter is for you.

Cortisol imbalance does more than just affect your body—it impacts your mind, your mood, and how connected you feel to yourself and the world around you. Chronic stress can rob you of motivation, blur your sense of identity, and make you feel like you're trapped under a constant weight. But that is not who you are. That is just what stress has done to you. And the good news is that with the right reset, your spark can come back.

This chapter will walk you through how cortisol impacts your emotional life, and how this **21**-day plan can gently guide you back to yourself—clearer, calmer, and more confident than before.

The Emotional Cost of Cortisol Imbalance

Cortisol is often thought of as the stress hormone, but its role is much broader. It affects neurotransmitters in your brain that control mood, memory, and motivation. When cortisol stays elevated over time, it can disrupt your serotonin and dopamine levels, which are key to emotional stability and drive. You might find yourself crying more easily, losing patience over small things, or withdrawing from people and activities you used to enjoy.

At the same time, high cortisol lowers your resilience. Everyday problems can start to feel overwhelming. Decisions become harder. You may feel like you're spinning your wheels or walking through life in a fog. This is not a character flaw. It's your nervous system calling for help.

Hormonal survival mode is not just physical—it is deeply emotional. And until that stress signal gets turned down, no amount of willpower or positive thinking can restore the mental clarity and motivation you once had.

Why You Feel Disconnected From Yourself

One of the most painful aspects of hormone-related burnout is the loss of identity. You may look in the mirror and not recognize the woman staring back. You may wonder why everything feels harder now—why joy feels flat, why goals feel unreachable, why you have lost touch with the person you used to be.

This disconnection often begins with exhaustion and builds over time. You start saying no to things you once loved because you are too tired. You stop dressing up, laughing loudly, or planning for the future. You stop dreaming. Slowly, without even realizing it, you begin to disappear under layers of stress and survival. But you are still there. She is still in you. And your body knows the way back.

Restoring Emotional Stability

During this **21**-day reset, you will begin to see your mood shift—not because you are forcing it, but because you are finally addressing the internal chemistry that controls how you feel. As your blood sugar stabilizes, your brain fog lifts. As inflammation comes down, your anxiety softens. As your cortisol lowers, your serotonin rises. These changes are not just noticeable—they are life-giving.

You may find yourself laughing again without effort. You may notice you are less reactive. You may begin waking up with a new sense of calm. These are signs that your nervous system is healing. That you are no longer stuck in survival. That your emotions are returning to a grounded, balanced place.

Reclaiming Your Motivation

One of the most frustrating symptoms of burnout is the loss of drive. You want to care. You want to make changes. But you can't seem to move. Your to-do list grows, but your energy shrinks. This is not laziness. It is the freeze response—your body's way of conserving energy when it feels overwhelmed or depleted.

Over these **21** days, you will slowly rebuild your capacity for action. With better sleep, more nourishing meals, and nervous system support, your motivation will begin to return. Not as a jolt of pressure, but as a quiet readiness. You'll start wanting to take care of yourself again. You'll find joy in progress, not just in perfection. And you'll begin to trust your own ability to show up for your life, one small step at a time.

Confidence Rooted in Hormone Balance

Hormone-driven confidence is different from surface-level self-esteem. It is not about appearances or achievements. It is about internal safety. When your hormones are balanced, your body stops constantly scanning for danger. Your mind feels clearer. You can speak without second-guessing. You can rest without guilt. You can look in the mirror and see a woman who is grounded, capable, and whole—not perfect, but present.

This kind of confidence does not come from external changes. It grows from within. It is what happens when your body is not at war with itself. It is what happens when you feel stable, nourished, and calm in your own skin.

Welcoming Yourself Back

By the end of this plan, you may not have everything figured out—but you will feel more like yourself again. You'll have the tools to stay grounded on hard days, the energy to enjoy your life, and the emotional strength to keep moving forward.

You'll feel proud of how far you've come, not just because of the physical results, but because of the deeper healing taking place.

This chapter is not a promise that every moment will be easy. But it is a promise that the woman you used to be—the one who felt hopeful, strong, connected, and alive—she is not gone. She is waiting. And she is closer than you think.

You are not broken. You are healing. And you are finding your way home.

PART II: THE 5-TRIGGER DETOX PROTOCOL

The CORE Method & 5-Trigger Reset Explained

If cortisol dysregulation is the problem, rhythm is the solution. Your body isn't fighting you—it's trying to survive. And the only way out of survival mode is by sending consistent signals of safety. That's where the CORE Method and the **5**-Trigger Reset Protocol come in.

You don't need to overhaul your entire life overnight. You need to shift five daily rhythms that directly affect your nervous system, metabolism, and hormone balance. These triggers are practical, sustainable, and rooted in your biology—not in willpower or discipline.

Before we dive into the **5** triggers, let's start with the CORE framework.

What Is the CORE Method?

CORE stands for:

- Calm
- Optimize
- Rhythm
- Energy

These four words form the pillars of recovery from cortisol burnout. They're not just abstract ideas—they're daily practices that guide how you eat, move, rest, and respond to stress.

Let's look at each one:

1. Calm – Regulate Your Nervous System

Before any healing can happen, your body needs to feel safe. That starts with calming your overactive stress response. In survival mode, your sympathetic nervous system (fight-or-flight) stays dominant. This means digestion, reproduction, immune defense, and even sleep are deprioritized.

To begin recovery, your parasympathetic nervous system (rest and repair) needs to be reactivated. That doesn't require long meditations or spa days. It's about simple, accessible signals: slowing your breath, creating moments of stillness, eating without distraction, stretching instead of sprinting.

2. Optimize – Support Your Hormones and Metabolism

You don't need to micromanage every hormone in your body. Instead, focus on the lifestyle habits that allow them to function properly. Balanced blood sugar, nutrient-dense meals, gentle movement, and consistent sleep patterns can help restore estrogen, progesterone, insulin, and thyroid function—without medication or extremes.

The body is self-correcting when given the right conditions. Optimization is about consistency, not perfection.

3. Rhythm – Align with Your Body's Internal Clock

Your body operates on a natural circadian rhythm—a **24**-hour clock that regulates sleep, hunger, energy, digestion, and even emotions. When this rhythm is disrupted by erratic meals, poor sleep, inconsistent movement, or artificial light, your hormones follow suit.

The CORE method helps you reestablish rhythm by eating at regular intervals, going to bed at similar times, and syncing activity with energy levels. Rhythm restores balance in the most sustainable way.

4. Energy – Rebuild Without Overdrive

Many women in burnout want more energy, so they try to generate it through stimulants, intense workouts, or pushing through exhaustion. But real energy isn't force—it's flow.

The energy pillar of the CORE method focuses on rebuilding your energy from the inside out. That means fueling your cells, resting your body, and giving yourself permission to recharge without guilt. Sustainable energy is created, not chased.

5-The Trigger Reset Protocol

Now that you understand the CORE foundation, let's explore the five key triggers that directly reset your cortisol patterns. These are the most powerful daily shifts you can make. They don't require expensive tools or a perfect routine—just small, intentional changes in how you treat your body.

Each of these five triggers corresponds to one or more parts of the CORE Method.

Trigger 1: Meal Timing (Calm + Rhythm)

What you eat matters—but when you eat can be just as powerful. Irregular eating patterns lead to blood sugar crashes, which spike cortisol and create a cycle of fatigue and cravings. Skipping meals or eating too little keeps your body in a constant state of energy uncertainty.

The **5**-Trigger Reset teaches you to eat within one hour of waking, to eat every **3–4** hours during the day, and to include protein, fat, and slow carbs in every meal. This stabilizes blood sugar, reduces cravings, and prevents the cortisol rollercoaster.

Reset action: Build your day around consistent, balanced meals—not just snacks or grazing.

Trigger 2: Nervous System Soothers (Calm)

Your nervous system is the gatekeeper for all healing. If you're constantly activated—rushing, multitasking, checking your phone, skipping rest—your body won't shift into repair mode. The smallest signals can help retrain your system to relax.

This includes deep breathing (especially exhaling slowly), warm baths, slow walks, humming, light stretching, grounding, and pausing before meals. None of these take more than a few minutes, but when practiced consistently, they lower cortisol in profound ways.

Reset action: Pick one **5**-minute calming ritual and repeat it daily.

Trigger 3: Gentle Movement (Energy + Optimize)

High-intensity exercise increases cortisol temporarily. In healthy bodies, that's fine. But in burnout, it compounds stress. Gentle, restorative movement not only preserves energy—it helps regulate cortisol.

This doesn't mean you stop moving. You shift how you move: walking, strength training with rest intervals, mobility work, and yoga. These approaches lower inflammation, improve insulin sensitivity, and support hormonal healing—without draining you.

Reset action: Swap out **2** high-intensity workouts per week for restorative movement.

Trigger 4: Light Exposure & Sleep Rhythm (Rhythm + Energy)

Your circadian rhythm controls cortisol. Morning sunlight raises cortisol naturally and supports energy. Darkness at night lowers it so melatonin can rise. But most people stay indoors during the day and stare at bright screens at night—flipping the entire rhythm.

To reset cortisol, aim for **10–15** minutes of sunlight in the morning, dim lights at night, and a consistent sleep schedule. Good sleep isn't just about hours—it's about timing and quality.

Reset action: Get natural light before **10** AM and turn off screens **1** hour before bed.

Trigger 5: Blood Sugar Awareness (Optimize)

Blood sugar spikes and crashes are among the biggest hidden drivers of high cortisol. Even "healthy" meals can destabilize blood sugar if they're not balanced with the right macronutrients. You don't need to count carbs—you need to balance your plate.

Each meal should have protein, fat, and fiber-rich carbs to slow digestion and reduce the blood sugar spike. This steadies energy, reduces cravings, and lowers cortisol over time.

Reset action: Build every meal with a protein-fat-fiber anchor. Example: salmon, roasted veggies, and avocado.

Putting It All Together

The CORE Method isn't about quick fixes or drastic rules. It's about daily recalibration. When you apply the **5**-Trigger Reset consistently, you send your body the message it's been waiting for: "You're safe now."

- Your cravings begin to quiet
- Your sleep becomes deeper
- Your belly starts to soften
- Your energy begins to rebuild
- Your mind clears

And all of this happens not because you forced it—but because you reset your rhythms.

You've tried pushing harder. Now, you're trying something smarter. This is the foundation of your reset—and the beginning of a new way to live in your body. Calm, connected, and finally in sync.

Nutritional Reset: What to Eat and When

The fastest way to tell your body it's safe isn't through supplements or intense plans—it's through food. The right meals, at the right times, stabilize blood sugar, calm your nervous system, and regulate cortisol. That's why the Nutritional Reset is one of the most powerful tools in your healing journey.

This is not about eating less. It's about eating with intention and rhythm, so your body stops running on survival mode and starts running on nourishment.

Why Meal Timing Matters

Your body thrives on predictable patterns. When meals are erratic or unbalanced, your blood sugar spikes and crashes. Each crash is a stress signal—and every stress signal triggers cortisol. That's why skipping breakfast, grazing all day, or relying on snacks instead of real meals can keep you stuck in fatigue, cravings, and belly fat.

Cortisol is meant to rise in the morning and slowly fall through the day. Meal timing should support that natural curve. Here's how:

Ideal Cortisol & Food Rhythm

Time of Day	What's Happening to Cortisol	What to Eat	Why It Works
7–9 AM	Cortisol peaks naturally	Protein + fat + complex carbs	Grounds your nervous system & balances blood sugar
12–1 PM	Cortisol stabilizes	Balanced lunch with fiber	Keeps energy steady & prevents afternoon crashes
3–4 PM	Cortisol starts to dip	Small snack with protein & fat	Prevents blood sugar dips & cravings
6–7 PM	Cortisol naturally drops	Light, nutrient-rich dinner	Supports digestion & keeps insulin low at night
8–9 PM	Melatonin rises, cortisol lowers	Optional: light protein bedtime snack	Helps prevent **3** AM wakeups from blood sugar drops

The Cortisol-Friendly Plate

Each meal should include three key components. This combination keeps blood sugar steady and prevents cortisol spikes throughout the day:

Component	Examples	Role in Cortisol Balance
Protein	Eggs, chicken, lentils, salmon, Greek yogurt, tofu	Stabilizes blood sugar & supports neurotransmitters
Healthy Fats	Avocado, olive oil, chia seeds, nuts, coconut	Slows digestion & reduces cravings
Complex Carbs	Sweet potato, quinoa, oats, berries, lentils	Provides steady energy & supports serotonin
Bonus: Fiber & Color	Leafy greens, cruciferous veggies, herbs, spices	Supports detox, digestion & inflammation

Sample Meal Framework

Use this as a flexible structure to build meals that keep your energy stable and your hormones in sync.

Breakfast (Within 1 hour of waking)

- **2** eggs scrambled in ghee
- ½ avocado
- **1** slice of sourdough toast or sweet potato

OR

- Overnight oats with chia seeds, almond butter, berries, and protein powder

Lunch (High protein + fiber)

- Grilled chicken bowl with quinoa, roasted broccoli, kale, tahini drizzle

OR

- Turkey lettuce wraps with hummus, carrots, cucumbers, and a side of fruit

Afternoon Snack (3–4 PM)

- Handful of almonds + a boiled egg
- Greek yogurt with flaxseed
- Hummus with veggie sticks

Dinner (Light, anti-inflammatory)

- Baked salmon with steamed asparagus, turmeric rice, olive oil drizzle

OR

- Stir-fried tofu and vegetables over cauliflower rice, sprinkled with sesame seeds

Optional Bedtime Snack (only if waking at 3 AM)

- A boiled egg
- Small banana with almond butter
- Turkey slices with cucumber

What to Avoid During a Reset

Some foods and habits keep cortisol levels high and disrupt healing. Aim to reduce or eliminate the following during your reset:

What to Avoid	Why
Skipping meals	Causes blood sugar crashes and cortisol spikes
Sugary cereals or snacks	Spike blood sugar and worsen cravings
Caffeine on an empty stomach	Increases cortisol production
Ultra-processed foods	Trigger inflammation and digestive stress
Low-carb diets during burnout	Deprive brain and body of steady energy

Fillable: My Nutritional Reset Tracker

Use the table below to plan your meals and observe how they affect your energy and mood.

Meal	What I Ate	How I Felt After (**1–10**)	Mood/Energy Notes
Breakfast			
Lunch			
Snack (PM)			
Dinner			
Bedtime snack			

When you start eating in rhythm, you'll notice subtle but powerful changes: fewer cravings, less bloating, better sleep, and a calmer mind. Your body starts to believe it's safe. And when your body feels safe, healing begins.

This is not a diet. It's a conversation with your biology. One meal at a time.

Metabolic Timing for Real Results

Your body is not just a machine that burns calories. It's a living system governed by hormonal rhythms, especially cortisol, insulin, melatonin, and hunger-regulating hormones like ghrelin and leptin. These rhythms don't just affect what your body does with food and movement—they determine when it's most effective to eat, rest, and move.

This is the concept of metabolic timing—aligning your habits with your body's natural hormonal schedule to boost fat loss, improve energy, and restore balance. When you time your meals, movement, and rest to sync with these rhythms, you stop fighting biology and start working with it.

Metabolic timing is a core part of the Cortisol Reset because it addresses one of the most overlooked problems in women's health: doing the right things at the wrong time.

Your Body Has a Clock—And It's Tied to Hormones

Every cell in your body follows a circadian rhythm. This **24**-hour internal clock regulates:

- Cortisol and melatonin (energy and sleep)
- Insulin sensitivity (blood sugar response)
- Digestive enzymes (nutrient breakdown)
- Hunger hormones (appetite regulation)
- Body temperature and repair functions

Ignoring this clock—by skipping meals, eating late at night, or overtraining at odd hours—disrupts hormone balance and keeps cortisol elevated.

Metabolic timing is not about obsessively tracking hours. It's about understanding your hormonal curve and using it to guide when you eat, move, and recover.

The Daily Cortisol & Metabolism Curve

Here's a simplified version of how your body functions across the day:

Time of Day	Hormonal Focus	Ideal Action
6–9 AM	Cortisol peaks, insulin sensitivity high	Eat a protein-rich breakfast; light movement
10 AM–**1** PM	Stable energy	Most focused work or demanding cognitive tasks
1–3 PM	Energy starts to dip	Balanced lunch; avoid sugary snacks
3–5 PM	Second cortisol dip	Light snack if needed; gentle movement
6–8 PM	Cortisol winds down, melatonin rises	Light dinner; wind-down begins
9–11 PM	Melatonin dominates	Screen-free relaxation; prepare for deep sleep

Metabolic Timing for Meals

The when of eating is just as important as the what. Here's how to time meals for maximum hormonal support:

1. Eat Within **60** Minutes of Waking

Your body needs fuel in the morning to shut down the overnight cortisol surge and stabilize blood sugar. Skipping breakfast keeps cortisol high and slows metabolism.

Best choices:

- Scrambled eggs with greens and sweet potato
- Overnight oats with protein powder and seeds
- Greek yogurt with berries and almond butter

2. Don't Skip or Delay Lunch

Midday is when your body is still efficient at metabolizing food. A protein-rich, fiber-filled lunch prevents that mid-afternoon crash and supports steady insulin levels.

Best choices:

- Grilled chicken or tofu bowl with rice and vegetables
- Lentil soup with avocado toast
- Turkey lettuce wraps with hummus and raw veggies

3. Avoid Late-Night Eating

As cortisol falls and melatonin rises in the evening, digestion naturally slows. Heavy or high-carb meals late at night can disrupt sleep, spike cortisol, and promote fat storage.

Dinner timing: Aim to eat at least **2**–**3** hours before bed

Light evening options:

- Baked salmon with steamed vegetables
- Stir-fried tofu and bok choy
- Zucchini noodles with turkey meatballs

Metabolic Timing for Movement

Exercise is essential—but when you do it matters more than most realize. High-intensity workouts at the wrong time can increase stress and worsen hormonal dysregulation.

Morning (**6**–**9** AM):

- Cortisol is naturally high, making this a great time for light cardio or gentle strength
- Avoid fasted HIIT if you're already in burnout

Late Morning to Early Afternoon (**10** AM–**2** PM):

- Ideal window for more intense activity, if your energy supports it

- Strength training or moderate workouts help build resilience

Evening (after **6** PM):

- Cortisol should be winding down, so avoid intense workouts
- Focus on stretching, yoga, or a walk after dinner to aid digestion and sleep

Metabolic Timing for Sleep & Recovery

Sleep isn't just about hours—it's about when you sleep. Going to bed between **9:30** and **10:30** PM supports the natural rise in melatonin and fall in cortisol. Staying up too late—especially with screens—delays this process, leads to cortisol spikes, and increases next-day fatigue and cravings.

A predictable bedtime and wake time—even on weekends—helps stabilize your metabolic clock. This reduces inflammation, improves fat metabolism, and strengthens the stress response.

Why This Works

When your actions are timed to match your biology, your body begins to:

- Burn fat more efficiently
- Crave less sugar
- Sleep deeper
- Recover faster
- Stabilize weight without obsession

You don't need to count every bite or overexert yourself to get results. You just need to rebuild the rhythm that's been lost.

This is what metabolic timing makes possible: living in sync with your biology, not against it. For women with cortisol imbalance, it's not a hack—it's a necessity.

Journal Prompt: Aligning with My Body Clock

1. What time do I usually eat breakfast? Is it within **60** minutes of waking?

____

2. When does my energy feel highest? When does it dip?

____

3. Do I often eat late at night? What triggers that behavior?

____

4. What time do I currently go to bed? Do I feel rested in the morning?

____

5. What is one shift I can make this week to align better with my body's rhythm?

Metabolic timing isn't about rules. It's about reconnection. Listen to your body, and it will show you the way back to balance. One day. One rhythm. One reset at a time.

Movement That Heals, Not Harms

You've been told that exercise is the answer. That if you want to lose weight, clear brain fog, or "feel better," you need to move more. Maybe you've tried high-intensity workouts, early morning bootcamps, or back-to-back cardio days. Maybe you pushed through exhaustion, believing that fatigue was a sign you weren't trying hard enough.

But what if the real reason you're not seeing results isn't because you're not moving enough—it's because you're moving in a way that harms instead of heals?

When your body is stuck in survival mode, exercise can either be a powerful reset signal or another stressor keeping you stuck. The difference isn't in the workout itself—it's in what your nervous system and hormones are ready to handle.

Exercise and Cortisol: The Missing Link

All movement temporarily raises cortisol. This is normal and healthy in a balanced body. But if your cortisol is already elevated—or if you're dealing with chronic stress, fatigue, or hormonal burnout—intense movement becomes one more signal of threat.

That **45**-minute HIIT session might spike your cortisol even higher, leading to:

- Energy crashes
- Bloating or inflammation
- Sugar cravings post-workout
- Poor sleep
- Increased belly fat
- Irritability or anxiety

You may leave the gym feeling accomplished—but your body is quietly sounding the alarm.

In burnout recovery, exercise should support healing, not prove discipline. You want movement that regulates your nervous system, not drains it.

Signs Your Workouts Might Be Harming You

If you answer "yes" to any of the following, your current exercise routine may be spiking cortisol:

- Do you feel exhausted instead of energized after workouts?
- Do you dread working out but feel guilty skipping it?
- Do you have trouble falling asleep or feel wired at night?
- Are you gaining or holding onto fat despite regular workouts?
- Do you feel ravenous or crave sugar after exercising?

These are not signs of weakness. They are hormonal red flags. Your body is asking for a different kind of movement—one that restores, not depletes.

What Movement Does for Healing

Movement is still essential during a cortisol reset, but the goal shifts. You're no longer exercising to burn calories—you're moving to:

- Improve blood flow and oxygen
- Regulate cortisol and insulin
- Support lymphatic drainage
- Stimulate serotonin and dopamine
- Signal your body that it's safe to rest and recover

Healing movement is about communication, not control. It teaches your body to return to parasympathetic (rest-and-digest) mode. Over time, it builds energy instead of borrowing it.

Movement Types That Soothe & Support Hormonal Balance

Here are types of movement that are especially effective for women in burnout recovery:

1. Walking

Low-impact, rhythmic, and incredibly therapeutic. Walking outdoors, especially in the morning light, resets your circadian rhythm and gently lowers cortisol.

Goal: **20–40** minutes daily, even broken into chunks.

2. Pilates & Functional Strength

Strength training improves insulin sensitivity and preserves muscle mass—two key factors in hormonal health. But go slow. Focus on bodyweight, light weights, and breathing.

Frequency: **2–3** times per week, max **30–40** minutes.

3. Gentle Yoga or Stretching

Yoga soothes the nervous system, improves digestion, and reduces inflammation. Yin, restorative, or slow flow styles are ideal.

Use: As a recovery day, evening wind-down, or post-meal reset.

4. Mobility & Joint Care

Simple mobility routines improve movement patterns and reduce physical stress, especially in women who sit for most of the day.

Use: **5–10** minutes daily, even during work breaks.

5. Rebounding or Dance

Playful movement lowers cortisol and increases joy hormones. It doesn't have to be structured—just intuitive and enjoyable.

Use: When you're feeling stiff, irritable, or unmotivated.

Rethinking "Results"

In the diet and fitness world, "results" usually mean visible change—weight loss, muscle tone, endurance. But during cortisol recovery, results are internal.

These are the new markers of success:

- You sleep through the night
- You no longer crash in the afternoon
- You feel calm after movement, not wired
- You enjoy your workouts again
- You stop dreading exercise
- You lose weight naturally, without pressure

Healing movement helps restore your trust in your body. You begin to notice its cues. You respond with care. And your body, in return, begins to soften, strengthen, and stabilize.

Sample Weekly Movement Plan for Healing

Day	Movement Focus
Monday	**30**-minute walk + **10**-minute stretch
Tuesday	Strength training (light weights, **30** min)
Wednesday	Restorative yoga (**20–30** min)
Thursday	Walk or light mobility
Friday	Strength training or Pilates
Saturday	Dance, hike, or playful movement
Sunday	Full rest or gentle stretch

The truth is: your body wants to move. It wants to stretch, flow, breathe, and express itself. But it does not want to be punished. In this season, your job is not to push harder—it's to listen more deeply.

Movement should feel like a gift, not a grind. When it does, you'll know you're finally moving in the direction of healing.

Nervous System Reset Tools: Breath, Stillness & Calm

Cortisol healing doesn't start with your diet or workouts. It starts with your nervous system. Until your body feels safe, no meal plan or supplement will stick. That's because cortisol is deeply tied to the part of your brain responsible for sensing threat—your autonomic nervous system.

When your nervous system is stuck in a constant state of alert, your body prioritizes survival over everything else: digestion, sleep, fertility, metabolism. You can be eating well and still feel exhausted, inflamed, and anxious if your system is locked in fight-or-flight mode.

Resetting this system doesn't require silence or spiritual retreats. It requires small, daily cues—especially breath, stillness, and calm body-based practices—that tell your brain: "I am safe. You can exhale now."

Understanding the Autonomic Nervous System

Your nervous system operates in two primary states:

System	State	Function
Sympathetic (fight/flight)	Alert, reactive, tense	Mobilizes energy for stress or danger
Parasympathetic (rest/digest)	Calm, grounded, connected	Supports digestion, recovery, sleep

In burnout, the sympathetic system becomes dominant. You stay alert all day, even during rest. Your digestion slows, your heart rate stays elevated, and your body doesn't shift into repair mode.

The goal of nervous system resetting is to activate your parasympathetic system. You're not turning off stress—you're teaching your body how to recover from it.

Tool 1: Breathwork (The Fastest Reset)

Your breath is one of the few tools that communicates directly with your nervous system. And unlike diet or sleep, it works instantly. When your breath is shallow and fast, your brain receives the signal: danger is present. When your breath is slow and deep, it hears: all is well.

Here are three simple breath tools:

1. 4-7-8 Breathing (Bedtime or Overwhelm Relief)

- Inhale through your nose for **4** seconds
- Hold for **7** seconds
- Exhale through your mouth for **8** seconds

Repeat for **4–6** rounds.

This slows your heart rate and helps shift from panic to peace.

2. Box Breathing (Midday Reset)

- Inhale for **4** seconds
- Hold for **4** seconds
- Exhale for **4** seconds
- Hold for **4** seconds

Repeat in a square rhythm for **1–2** minutes.

Used by athletes and military teams to regulate stress.

3. Physiological Sigh (Quickest Reset)

- Take a deep inhale
- Take a second shorter inhale on top
- Long slow exhale through the mouth

Repeat **2–3** times.

This instantly reduces physiological stress and balances CO_2.

When to use breathwork:

- Upon waking to ground your day
- Before meals to improve digestion
- After a stressor to calm tension
- Before bed to ease anxiety

Tool 2: Stillness Practices (Reset from Overstimulation)

Stillness doesn't mean doing nothing—it means intentionally creating space to unplug your body from constant external input.

1. Grounding

Sit or stand barefoot on grass, soil, or sand. Being physically connected to the earth has been shown to reduce inflammation and cortisol. Even **10** minutes counts.

2. Legs Up the Wall

Lie on your back with your legs elevated against a wall. Stay for **5–10** minutes. This calms the vagus nerve, improves circulation, and lowers heart rate.

3. Eyes Softened, Focus Softened

Lie or sit comfortably and let your eyes slightly blur. Avoid focusing on any one point. Let your gaze rest. This signals safety and reduces visual tension that often keeps the brain alert.

4. Silence

Take **5** minutes each day with no screens, no music, no talking. Just breathe and be. Your body will initially resist, but over time, this becomes one of the most grounding habits in your cortisol healing toolkit.

Tool 3: Micro-Calm Moments Throughout the Day

You don't need an hour to reset your nervous system. These are quick, nervous-system-friendly rituals you can build into your day:

Trigger Moment Reset Practice

Before meals	**3** deep breaths to calm digestion
After emails or meetings	One-minute hand massage
While standing in line	Gentle shoulder rolls or jaw release
Afternoon slump	Box breathing + look out a window
Evening wind-down	Candlelight stretch or warm compress

The more you stack these small resets into your day, the more you teach your body it doesn't need to stay "on" all the time.

The Real Power of Calm

Calm isn't a luxury—it's biology. And in cortisol recovery, calm is medicine. It's what signals your system to shift gears. These tools aren't optional extras. They're part of the core repair process. They restore trust between you and your body.

And over time, you'll notice:

- Your digestion improves
- Your heart rate settles
- You stop clenching your jaw or holding your breath
- Your sleep deepens
- Your cravings decrease
- Your energy steadies

Self Check-In: Your Nervous System Reset Toolkit

1. What's my current default state most of the day?

☐ Calm and grounded

☐ Rushed and tense

☐ Overstimulated and anxious

2. Which breathwork technique feels most approachable for me?

☐ **4-7-8** breathing

☐ Box breathing

☐ Physiological sigh

3. Which stillness practice can I try this week?

☐ Grounding outdoors

☐ Legs up the wall

☐ **5** minutes of silence

4. Where in my day can I insert a micro calm moment?

☐ Morning wake-up

☐ Midday reset

☐ Before meals

☐ Before bed

You don't need to meditate for an hour. You don't need to be zen all the time. You just need to interrupt the chronic stress signals—and these tools help you do that.

When your nervous system feels safe, your hormones follow. Calm is not weakness. It is your path back to clarity, strength, and health. One breath at a time.

Adaptogens & Supplements That Actually Work

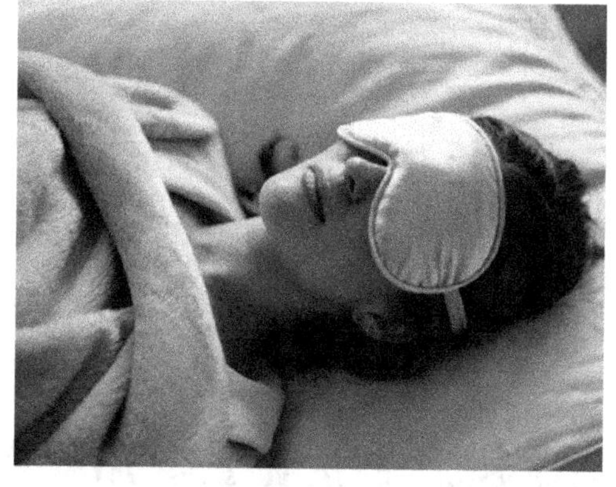

In the search for hormone balance and energy, many women turn to supplements hoping for fast relief—especially when sleep, digestion, mood, and metabolism feel out of control. But with so many pills, powders, and promises, it's easy to waste money, time, and hope on products that do nothing or worse, backfire.

This section cuts through the noise. It focuses on what actually works to support your cortisol, nervous system, and hormone recovery—particularly when you're stuck in survival mode. While no supplement replaces rest, food, and nervous system healing, the right ones can gently support your body's natural reset process.

What Are Adaptogens?

Adaptogens are natural substances—usually herbs or mushrooms—that help your body adapt to stress and restore balance. They don't force hormones up or down. Instead, they support your adrenal system in regulating cortisol and calming the stress response.

Think of adaptogens like buffers. When your cortisol is too high, they help bring it down. When it's too low, they support bringing it back up. Over time, they build resilience, not dependency.

Adaptogens are not stimulants. They're subtle, slow, and work best when taken consistently over weeks. Their power lies in their gentleness.

The Top Adaptogens for Cortisol Support

Adaptogen	Primary Benefit	Best For
Ashwagandha	Calms cortisol, improves sleep, reduces anxiety	Evening use, high cortisol symptoms
Rhodiola Rosea	Boosts energy, improves mood, enhances stamina	Fatigue, brain fog, low motivation
Holy Basil	Reduces mental stress, stabilizes blood sugar	Cravings, emotional overwhelm
Schisandra	Liver support, hormonal balance, reduces fatigue	Detox support, mental clarity
Reishi Mushroom	Deep nervous system regulation, supports sleep, immunity	Bedtime relaxation, immune fatigue
Eleuthero (Siberian Ginseng)	Increases stress resilience, combats fatigue	Early burnout recovery, immune support

Not all adaptogens are the same. Some are energizing, others calming. Choosing the right one for your current state is key. For example, if you're anxious and wired, Rhodiola might overstimulate you. But Reishi or Ashwagandha may feel like grounding support.

How to Take Adaptogens

- Start low and go slow. Half doses are a good place to begin.
- Take consistently for **3–6** weeks, then reassess.
- Cycle off for a week every **1–2** months.
- Avoid mixing too many adaptogens at once unless guided by a practitioner.
- Look for high-quality extracts (preferably organic, third-party tested).

Forms include capsules, tinctures, powders, and teas. Your choice depends on personal preference, but absorption is often higher in liquid forms.

Supplements That Support Cortisol & Nervous System Balance

Adaptogens are only part of the picture. Certain nutrients can also make a dramatic difference in recovery from cortisol dysregulation. Here are the essentials:

1. Magnesium (Glycinate or Malate)

Most people are deficient. Magnesium calms the nervous system, supports muscle recovery, improves sleep, and reduces anxiety.

- Dose: **200–400** mg at night
- Avoid: Magnesium oxide (poorly absorbed)

2. Vitamin C

Your adrenal glands use a lot of vitamin C when under stress. It helps lower cortisol, supports immune function, and reduces oxidative damage.

- Dose: **500–1000** mg daily with food
- Form: Ascorbate or liposomal forms are ideal

3. B Complex Vitamins

B**6**, B**12**, and folate are vital for mood, energy, and hormone metabolism. Stress depletes them quickly.

- Look for: "Active" forms like methylcobalamin (B**12**) and P-**5**-P (B**6**)
- Avoid: Cheap, synthetic forms like cyanocobalamin

4. L-Theanine

Found naturally in green tea, L-theanine promotes a calm, focused state without drowsiness. It balances cortisol, sharpens concentration, and reduces racing thoughts.

- Dose: **100–200** mg as needed
- Use: Before stressful events or in the afternoon to ease tension

5. Omega-**3** Fatty Acids

Omega-**3**s reduce inflammation, improve mood, and support brain and hormone health. They also help regulate the HPA (hypothalamic-pituitary-adrenal) axis—the system that governs cortisol output.

- Dose: **1000–2000** mg combined EPA/DHA daily
- Source: Fish oil or algae oil for plant-based options

What to Avoid

Some supplements are marketed as helpful but often worsen cortisol dysregulation, especially if you're already burnt out.

- High-dose caffeine-based fat burners - overstimulate adrenals
- Excess green tea extract - can increase anxiety in sensitive people
- Pre-workouts - spike cortisol and disrupt blood sugar
- Overuse of melatonin - may blunt your body's natural rhythm long-term

Always read labels carefully. Just because it's natural doesn't mean it's right for your current state.

Final Thoughts

Adaptogens and supplements aren't magic bullets. But when chosen wisely, they can offer profound support—especially when combined with real food, proper sleep, and nervous system regulation.

The most powerful supplements are the ones that help your body do what it's already trying to do: find balance.

In burnout recovery, the goal is never to push harder—it's to support deeper. With the right support, your body doesn't just stabilize. It begins to thrive. Quietly, steadily, from the inside out.

Emotional Support and Cortisol-Friendly Mindset Shifts

Your thoughts and emotions aren't just feelings floating in your head—they're deeply physical. Every moment of anxiety, guilt, perfectionism, or pressure sends real signals to your body, triggering real stress responses. Cortisol doesn't rise only because of external events. It rises when your mind interprets life as unsafe, urgent, or overwhelming.

That's why emotional support and mindset shifts are not "extras" in a cortisol reset. They're essential. If you've ever done all the right things—ate clean, exercised gently, took your supplements—and still felt anxious, inflamed, or stuck, the missing piece might not be food. It might be your inner dialogue.

Let's explore the emotional traps that keep cortisol high, and the mindset shifts that can finally bring relief.

The Emotional Patterns That Keep You in Survival Mode

Certain thought loops signal your nervous system to stay in a state of alert. These patterns are common in high-achieving women and often go unnoticed:

1. Perfectionism

Believing that everything must be done exactly right—or else. This leads to constant self-surveillance, anxiety, and pressure. Even when your body is tired, your mind says, "Keep going."

2. People-Pleasing

Saying yes when you want to say no. Feeling responsible for everyone's happiness. This drains emotional energy, creates resentment, and tells your body it's never allowed to rest.

3. Catastrophizing

Always expecting the worst. Worrying that one bad day, one skipped workout, or one slip-up will ruin everything. This fuels hypervigilance and panic-mode cortisol spikes.

4. Self-Criticism

Telling yourself you're lazy, undisciplined, or not good enough. This keeps your brain in a constant fight-or-flight relationship with your own body.

These emotional patterns aren't flaws. They're adaptive behaviors you may have learned to stay safe, get approval, or meet impossible standards. But now, they're exhausting you.

Cortisol-Friendly Mindset Shifts

To reset cortisol, you must not only calm your body—but also change the story your mind is telling. Here are practical mindset shifts to help rewire your internal world:

1. From: "I have to do everything right."

To: "Consistency matters more than perfection."

Your body doesn't need perfection—it needs steady rhythms. A missed workout, a late night, or a hard week won't undo your progress. The goal is pattern, not precision.

2. From: "I'm not doing enough."

To: "Rest is a form of productivity."

Rest is when healing happens. It's not lazy. It's not optional. It's how your hormones reset, how your mind recovers, and how your energy returns.

3. From: "I failed again."

To: "Every symptom is a signal, not a failure."

That craving, that irritability, that fatigue—it's not failure. It's feedback. Your body is talking to you, not rebelling. When you listen without judgment, you begin to heal.

4. From: "I need to be in control."

To: "I can trust my body."

Control often comes from fear. Trust comes from rhythm. As you build supportive habits, your body will respond—and you'll no longer need to micromanage it.

Emotional Self-Support Practices

Beyond thoughts, emotional regulation tools help lower cortisol in real time. Here are a few to incorporate regularly:

- Name what you feel. Say out loud: "I feel anxious," or "I feel tired and sad today." Naming reduces overwhelm and engages the rational brain.
- Place a hand on your chest or belly. Physical touch signals safety and soothes the nervous system.
- Use a calming mantra. Try: "I am safe. I don't have to rush. My body is allowed to rest."

- Create emotional boundaries. If something drains you repeatedly—news, a certain relationship, social media—give yourself permission to step away.

Final Thought

You are not just healing your hormones. You are retraining your mind to live in safety instead of survival. The thoughts you choose, the boundaries you set, the grace you offer yourself—all of it matters. It shapes your biology.

Your reset is not just physical. It's emotional. And your nervous system is listening. Every time you soften, breathe, and say, "It's okay to rest," your body exhales with you. That's where healing begins.

PART III: YOUR 21-DAY CORTISOL DETOX PLAN

Week 1: Calm the System & Reduce Inflammation

This first week is all about doing less, but doing it with intention. If you have been running on empty, pushing through fatigue, and wondering why your body will not respond to healthy habits, it is not your fault. Your nervous system has likely been in survival mode for too long. Cortisol, the hormone your body uses to respond to stress, has probably been stuck on high. You may feel wired but tired, bloated, anxious, or just plain worn out. That is not a lack of discipline. It is a sign your body is stuck in defense.

This week, we begin gently interrupting that stress cycle. The goal is not to work harder or eat less. It is to calm the system, lower internal stress, and reduce inflammation. That is the true starting point for weight loss, better sleep, and a renewed sense of self. You are building a foundation that everything else will grow from. Take it seriously and treat yourself with kindness.

Priority 1: Calm the Nervous System

Your body does not respond to ideas. It responds to signals. You cannot just tell yourself to relax and expect your system to follow. You have to show your nervous system, through action and consistency, that it is safe to relax. The brain needs evidence, not theory.

These small daily habits are powerful. They gently guide your body out of fight or flight and into rest and recovery.

Daily calming practices:

- Start your day without your phone. Instead of reaching for a screen, spend two quiet minutes breathing, stretching, or simply sitting with your thoughts.
- Practice **4-7-8** breathing at least twice a day. Inhale for **4** seconds, hold for **7**, exhale for **8**. Repeat for three rounds to calm your system.
- Schedule one five-minute pause during your day. This can be closing your eyes, doing legs-up-the-wall, stepping outside for fresh air, or just resting quietly.

These are not extra tasks. They are the reset. Do not skip them. They are how your body learns to trust again.

Priority 2: Reduce Inflammation Through Food

Cortisol and blood sugar are closely connected. When blood sugar drops, cortisol rises. That is why skipping meals, eating sugar-heavy snacks, or surviving on caffeine keeps your system on edge. Stabilizing your meals is one of the fastest ways to stabilize your mood, energy, and metabolism.

Daily eating rhythm:

- Eat within one hour of waking to prevent a morning cortisol surge.
- Eat every **3** to **4** hours. Skipping meals makes your body feel unsafe.
- Include protein, fat, and fiber in every meal to support blood sugar balance.
- Stay hydrated throughout the day. Even mild dehydration raises cortisol.

Anti-inflammatory meal upgrades:

- Avoid ultra-processed foods, refined sugar, and industrial seed oils.
- Include calming, anti-inflammatory foods like turmeric, ginger, leafy greens, berries, and wild-caught fish.
- Reduce alcohol and caffeine, especially in the afternoon and evening.
- If you notice bloating, skin irritation, or digestive issues, limit dairy and gluten to see if symptoms improve.

This is not about perfection. It is about creating a stable, nourishing rhythm. Every meal is a message to your hormones: we are safe, we are fed, we can rest.

Movement This Week: Gentle and Restorative

If your system is stressed, intense workouts can make it worse. This week, we focus on calm, steady movement.

- Take one walk a day. Even **10** or **20** minutes is enough.
- Avoid high-intensity exercise. No sprints, bootcamps, or fast cardio sessions.
- Do light stretching or mobility exercises, especially before bed. Just five minutes helps lower cortisol and ease tension.

Movement is not about burning calories this week. It is about calming your body and building consistency. Walking, stretching, and breathing are your tools. Use them.

Mindset for Week 1: Less Is Enough

You might wonder if this is really doing anything. You might feel the urge to push harder or do more. Resist it. The healing you are starting is quiet. It works under the surface. But it is powerful.

You are not being lazy. You are giving your body a chance to reset. That is the bravest and most productive thing you can do right now. If your body has been in high alert for years, rest is not a reward. It is the treatment.

Weekly Checklist:

- Eat breakfast within **60** minutes of waking
- Include protein, fat, and fiber in every meal
- Do breathwork twice a day
- Walk at least three times this week
- Practice one calming ritual before bed each night

You are not falling behind. You are meeting yourself where you are. Let the calm begin. Week **2** will build on this solid foundation.

Week 2: Reset Rhythm – Sleep, Sugar and Cravings

You made it through Week **1**, and now your body is beginning to notice something different. The noise has quieted a little. You may feel slightly calmer, less bloated, and more grounded. That's the result of the consistent safety signals you've been sending. Now, in Week **2**, we build on that foundation by creating rhythm. Rhythm is what your body craves more than perfection. This is the week we focus on stabilizing your sleep cycle, balancing your blood sugar, and reducing those intense cortisol-driven cravings that often feel impossible to control.

This week is not about doing everything flawlessly. It is about creating a steady, reliable rhythm that your hormones can depend on. When cortisol knows what to expect, it starts to drop naturally. That is what allows weight loss, emotional balance, and better sleep to take root.

Priority 1: Stabilize Your Blood Sugar

Unstable blood sugar is one of the fastest ways to spike cortisol. Every time your glucose drops too low, your body sees it as an emergency and pumps out more stress hormones. That is why you might feel anxious, lightheaded, shaky, or suddenly irritable before meals. By smoothing out those peaks and valleys, we help your system stay calm and focused.

Daily practices for blood sugar balance:

- Keep eating every **3** to **4** hours, even if you are not very hungry
- Never skip meals, especially breakfast
- Start meals with protein and fiber before moving to carbs
- If you crave sugar, pause and check in with yourself first. You may be tired, thirsty, or under-eating earlier in the day

If you feel hungry all the time, it is not a lack of willpower. It is often a hormone imbalance. Stabilizing meals with the right foods at the right times will begin to fix that.

Priority 2: Improve Sleep Quality

Last week, we began calming your nervous system. Now, we focus directly on restoring your sleep cycle. Good sleep is not just about how many hours you get. It is about how deeply you rest and how consistently you sleep through the night.

Steps to improve sleep:

- Keep a consistent bedtime and wake time, even on weekends
- Get sunlight on your skin within one hour of waking to reset your circadian rhythm
- Eat a protein-rich breakfast to signal morning energy to your brain
- Reduce screens, bright lights, and stimulating tasks two hours before bed
- Try a small bedtime snack with protein and fat to prevent **3** AM cortisol spikes

You may already notice small improvements. If not, do not worry. Sleep takes time to repair. You are not doing it wrong. Keep the rhythm, and results will come.

Priority 3: Reduce Cravings and Emotional Eating

Cortisol is a craving hormone. When it is high, your brain looks for quick fuel. That is why you crave carbs, sugar, and salty snacks when you are stressed or tired. It is a survival response, not a character flaw. The solution is not to fight the cravings. It is to understand and replace the pattern.

Tips to reduce cravings:

- Do not let yourself get too hungry. Under-eating is the biggest driver of rebound cravings
- Drink water between meals to avoid confusing thirst with hunger
- Use the **5**-minute rule. When a craving hits, wait five minutes, take a breath, and ask yourself what you really need
- Replace quick-fix snacks with real nourishment. Try boiled eggs, nut butter on apple slices, or roasted sweet potatoes

You do not need to eliminate all treats. But this week is about replacing stress snacking with intentional nourishment. This is how you shift from reaction to rhythm.

Movement This Week: Gentle Consistency

You are still in healing mode, but by now your energy may be starting to return. If you feel ready, increase your walks or try adding light bodyweight movement like squats, lunges, or yoga flows. Keep listening to your body. Movement should leave you feeling better, not depleted.

Movement goals:

- Walk five days this week, even short walks count
- Add in one or two ten-minute strength or flow sessions if you feel energized
- Stretch or breathe before bed to signal wind-down

Mindset for Week 2: Choose Rhythm Over Intensity

You do not need to hustle harder. You need to stay steady. Your body is learning what it feels like to feel safe again. That takes rhythm, not punishment. If you feel like you are doing less than usual, remind yourself that less can be more, especially when it is consistent.

Healing is not always dramatic. Often it is quiet. A deeper night of sleep. A day with fewer cravings. A moment where you feel calm for no reason. These are not small. They are signs that the shift is happening.

Weekly Checklist:

- Eat every **3** to **4** hours
- Get sunlight exposure within one hour of waking
- Wind down with no screens two hours before bed
- Walk at least five times this week
- Have one calming bedtime routine each night
- Practice **4**-**7**-**8** breathing daily
- Journal your sleep and energy levels to track progress

You are building rhythm now. And rhythm builds resilience. Let Week **2** be a time of trust, nourishment, and steady progress. Week **3** will guide you into rebuilding energy and reclaiming the motivation that may have felt out of reach. Keep going. You are doing beautifully.

Week 3: Rebuild Energy and Reclaim Confidence

Welcome to Week **3**. By now, your body has received something it may not have experienced in a long time—consistency, calm, and nourishment. The survival mode that once kept you tense, anxious, and exhausted is finally beginning to loosen its grip. You may have already noticed improvements in your sleep, fewer cravings, or a clearer mind. These are signs that your hormones are beginning to trust you again.

This week, we focus on rebuilding energy, restoring motivation, and reconnecting with the version of you that feels confident and steady. You are no longer just getting through the day. You are starting to move forward with clarity and purpose. Week **3** is about stepping into that momentum.

Priority 1: Support Natural Energy

Real energy does not come from caffeine, sugar, or sheer willpower. It comes from balanced hormones, stable blood sugar, quality sleep, and a regulated nervous system. This week, we focus on sustaining energy throughout the day, without crashes or stimulation.

Daily energy practices:

- Eat a full breakfast within one hour of waking to support cortisol balance
- Continue eating every **3** to **4** hours to avoid energy dips
- Begin your day with natural light and movement, even **5** minutes of stretching or walking helps
- Avoid caffeine on an empty stomach, and reduce intake after **12** PM
- Stay hydrated with water and mineral-rich drinks like herbal teas or lemon water

If you feel tired in the afternoon, pause and assess. Are you under-eating? Overthinking? Overworking? The solution may not be to push through. It may be to take a break, nourish yourself, and come back stronger.

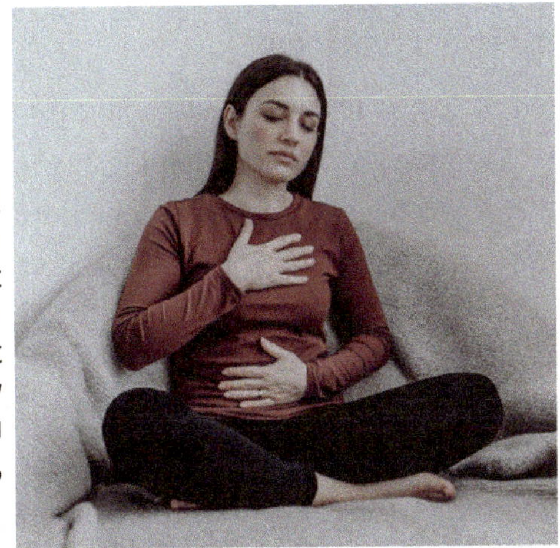

Priority 2: Reignite Motivation

Burnout steals motivation. High cortisol makes your brain prioritize short-term survival over long-term goals. That is why you may have lost interest in hobbies, stopped setting goals, or felt flat for months or even years. But now that your stress response is calming, you are in a better place to rebuild desire, drive, and direction.

How to reignite motivation:

- Set one small goal each morning. It could be a walk, a nourishing lunch, or ten minutes of reading. Keep it doable.
- Celebrate wins, even tiny ones. Finished a walk? Drank enough water? Slept well? Acknowledge it.
- Choose progress over pressure. Don't chase perfection. Focus on the direction you're going.

Motivation returns when your body no longer feels like it's fighting for survival. It begins when you treat yourself with kindness and curiosity.

Priority 3: Reconnect with Confidence

Confidence is not about appearance or achievement. It is about feeling steady in your mind and safe in your body. As cortisol lowers, your sense of self becomes clearer. You may start dressing differently, speaking up more, or feeling more connected to the world around you. These changes are not superficial. They are the result of healing.

Confidence-building habits:

- Journal about one thing each day that made you feel strong, proud, or calm
- Reflect on the changes you have noticed since starting the plan
- Speak kindly to yourself. If a critical thought comes up, reframe it with compassion

You are not returning to the "old" you. You are meeting a wiser, more grounded version of yourself. Confidence is already within you. You are simply uncovering it.

Movement This Week: Energizing and Empowering

Now that your energy is more stable, you can explore movement that feels good and builds strength. You are not exercising to burn calories. You are moving to celebrate your body's capacity and build resilience.

Movement suggestions:

- Continue daily walks, aiming for **20** to **30** minutes if possible
- Add light strength training or yoga **2** to **3** times this week
- Stretch every evening to support deep sleep and muscle recovery

Let movement remind you that your body is capable, adaptable, and worth caring for.

Mindset for Week 3: You Are Moving Forward

You may not have reached every goal. That is okay. You have already made powerful shifts in your body and mind. You are eating with more clarity. You are sleeping with more ease. You are moving through your day with more awareness. That is success.

Progress is not always visible right away. But the foundation you've built over the past three weeks is changing how your body responds to stress, how your brain processes emotion, and how your hormones work behind the scenes. Trust that the changes will continue.

Weekly Checklist:

- Eat a nourishing breakfast within **60** minutes of waking
- Continue eating balanced meals every **3** to **4** hours
- Walk at least five times this week
- Try two strength or yoga sessions if your energy allows
- Journal your wins and emotional shifts daily
- Do one thing this week just for joy or fun
- Practice one evening ritual to support deep sleep

This is not the end. It is a new beginning. You are not just healing your hormones. You are rebuilding trust with yourself. You are showing your body and mind that it is safe to thrive. And that is the most powerful transformation of all.

Emergency Fixes: What to Do When You Can't Sleep, Crave Sugar, or Feel Exhausted

No matter how well you plan, real life happens. You will have nights when you can't fall asleep, afternoons when your sugar cravings feel overwhelming, and days when you feel completely drained. That doesn't mean you're failing or falling behind. It means you're human. This chapter is here to meet you in those moments—without judgment, without pressure, and with practical tools that bring quick relief.

You don't need to do everything perfectly to heal. You just need to know how to support yourself when things feel off. The following emergency fixes are designed for those exact situations when you feel stuck, frustrated, or unsure what your body is asking for.

Each section will walk you through what's happening behind the scenes, what your body is likely signaling, and what you can do in that moment to feel better—gently and effectively.

When You Can't Sleep

What's likely happening:

Your cortisol may be spiking when it should be dropping. This can happen if your blood sugar dips too low during the night, if your brain is overstimulated, or if your nervous system is still in high-alert mode when you go to bed.

What to try:

1. Eat a small, calming bedtime snack

A mix of protein and healthy fat helps prevent nighttime cortisol spikes. Try half a banana with almond butter, a hard-boiled egg, or a small piece of turkey with avocado. If you've gone to bed hungry, your body may wake you up in the middle of the night.

2. Do **4-7-8** breathing

If your mind is racing, this breathing technique helps calm your nervous system quickly. Inhale for **4** seconds, hold for **7**, exhale for **8**. Repeat three to four times. Do it lying down or even sitting upright if needed.

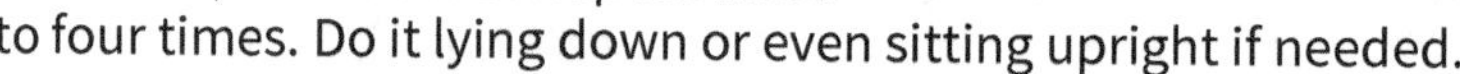

3. Use a grounding sensory tool

Sometimes your brain needs to shift away from the mental chatter. Try placing one hand over your heart and one on your belly. Feel the rise and fall of your breath. You can also press your feet into the mattress or count backwards from **100** to redirect your focus.

4. Get out of bed for a few minutes

If you've been lying awake for more than **20–30** minutes, get up and do something calming in low light. Read a physical book, stretch gently, or journal. Avoid screens, bright lights, or checking the time repeatedly.

5. Magnesium or herbal support

If you're still struggling, try sipping on warm magnesium tea or a cortisol-calming herbal blend like chamomile, lemon balm, or passionflower. These won't knock you out, but they can ease the edge and help your body transition into rest.

When You Crave Sugar

What's likely happening:

Your cortisol is pushing you to seek fast fuel. That can be caused by a blood sugar drop, skipped meals, poor sleep, or emotional stress. Sugar cravings are not a failure. They are a signal.

What to try:

1. Ask yourself: "Did I eat enough earlier?"

Cravings often come when you haven't had enough protein or fat throughout the day. If you've skipped breakfast or had a low-protein lunch, your body may be asking for quick energy now. Start with a balanced snack instead of going straight to sugar.

2. Drink water with a pinch of salt or a splash of lemon

Dehydration can amplify cravings and make you feel more fatigued. Add minerals to your water to help rehydrate at the cellular level and support your adrenal function.

3. Replace with a satisfying alternative

Have a handful of berries with Greek yogurt, dark chocolate with almond butter, or a date with cashew cream. You're not depriving yourself—you're upgrading the fuel.

4. Do a five-minute nervous system reset

Cravings are often tied to emotion. Try this: sit quietly, place your hands on your thighs, and take slow, deep breaths. Remind your body that you are not in danger. Then, if you still want the treat, enjoy it slowly and mindfully.

5. Reframe the craving

Instead of thinking, "I'm weak," try, "My body is asking for support." That shift removes guilt and gives you power to respond with care.

When You Feel Exhausted

What's likely happening:

Your cortisol may be tanking after being high for too long, or your blood sugar may be unstable. Emotional or mental stress can also create real physical fatigue. Instead of pushing through, give your body what it is truly asking for.

What to try:

1. Eat a stabilizing mini-meal

A mix of protein, fat, and fiber can restore your energy without a crash. Try a boiled egg with carrots, hummus and crackers, or a chia pudding with almond milk and berries. If you're tired and wired, your body may actually be under-fueled.

2. Do a posture reset

Sit upright and roll your shoulders back. Slouching can compress your lungs and signal low energy to your brain. Take five deep breaths into your lower ribs. This one-minute fix often brings a noticeable shift.

3. Move your body gently

Even if you feel drained, a short walk or a few minutes of stretching can improve circulation and wake up your brain. Movement increases energy when done gently and intentionally.

4. Step away from stimulation

Bright screens, multitasking, and background noise can drain your energy quickly. Take a short break in silence, close your eyes, or step outside. Nature is a fast-acting nervous system reset, even if it's just fresh air.

5. Give yourself permission to rest

If you've been pushing all day, your exhaustion may be a sign that you need to stop. Rest is productive when your body is healing. A **20**-minute nap, lying down without a screen, or even closing your eyes for a few minutes can restore more than another hour of grinding through fatigue.

General Tips When You Feel Off Track

You will have days where things feel messy. Maybe you overdid it, snapped at someone, skipped meals, or had three coffees before noon. That's okay. Healing is not about perfection. It is about response.

When you feel off:

- Breathe first. One slow exhale signals your brain that you are in control.
- Reconnect to rhythm. Eat your next meal, walk for a few minutes, drink some water.
- Remind yourself that one hard day does not erase your progress.
- Go to bed early. Most things feel better after rest.

You do not have to fix everything at once. You just need to do the next nourishing thing. And then the next.

Final Note

These emergency fixes are not just quick tools. They are practice in self-compassion. When you respond gently to your body, it begins to trust you. When your body trusts you, it lets go of tension, inflammation, and resistance.

You are not stuck. You are learning new ways to care for yourself. Some days will feel smooth, others will be bumpy. But now you have a map. You know how to respond with calm, not panic. You know how to meet your needs without guilt. And most importantly, you are learning that the path to healing is not harsh. It is kind.

Keep this section nearby. Use it when things feel off. Return to it anytime you forget how far you have come. Your body is not the enemy. It is the messenger. And with the right support, it is fully capable of returning to balance, strength, and peace.

After-Detox Reset for Lasting Weight Loss & Sleep Rhythm

Finishing the reset is a major achievement. You've invested in calming your nervous system, stabilizing blood sugar, and shifting your body out of survival mode. But now comes the most important part of all. Building a life that supports your cortisol rhythm every day, not just during a structured program.

You do not need to maintain every habit you learned. You do need to protect the core rhythms that tell your body it is safe. A cortisol-friendly lifestyle is not about strict rules or flawless routines. It is about living with awareness and returning to balance as often as possible.

Reframe the Goal

A long-term cortisol-friendly life is not about constant progress or perfection. It is about maintenance and reconnection. Instead of asking "How do I fix this?" shift to asking "What helps me stay regulated?"

Regulated means:

- Your sleep is predictable and restorative
- Your meals feel nourishing and steady
- You move your body without exhaustion
- Your emotions feel like information, not emergencies
- You recover from stress without spiraling

These are the true markers of success. Not your weight. Not your step count. Not your productivity. A regulated body is a healthy body, even before it looks different.

Anchor Your Day with Cortisol-Supportive Rhythms

Your cortisol still follows a natural **24**-hour rhythm. Help it stay in sync by reinforcing daily anchors. These are small but powerful habits that give your body consistency.

Morning

- Wake around the same time every day, including weekends
- Get natural sunlight within **30** minutes of waking
- Eat a breakfast with protein, fat, and slow carbs
- Avoid phone or email in the first **20** minutes

Midday

- Eat lunch before **1** PM
- Take a movement break after eating, even a **10**-minute walk
- Drink water with minerals or add herbal tea for hydration

Evening

- Eat dinner at least **2** to **3** hours before bed
- Dim lights and reduce screen use after sunset
- Practice a wind-down ritual such as stretching, reading, or breathwork
- Get in bed by **10** or **10**:**30** PM if possible

These rhythms may not happen every single day. That is not the goal. The goal is to return to them more often than not.

Build a Resilient Relationship with Food

Your body thrives when it knows nourishment is coming. Keep food supportive and simple.

Foundational guidelines

- Eat every **3** to **4** hours
- Include protein, fat, and fiber in every meal
- Choose foods that leave you feeling steady, not spiked
- Use snacks to support energy dips, not replace meals

Avoid diets that force your body into restriction or survival mode. A long-term cortisol-friendly diet is flexible, gentle, and nutrient-rich. You can enjoy treats. You can eat out. You can make choices based on how you feel, not what a chart says.

Food is not a threat. It is a tool for rhythm and regulation.

Move to Regulate, Not Punish

Exercise should support your energy, not deplete it. You do not need to follow a perfect routine. You need movement that keeps your body mobile, your hormones balanced, and your nervous system grounded.

Cortisol-friendly movement plan

- Walk daily, even for **15** to **30** minutes
- Strength train **2** to **3** times per week with good recovery
- Use yoga, Pilates, or stretching for active rest
- Avoid intense training when sleep or energy is low

If movement ever feels like pressure or punishment, scale back. Respect your current state. Movement should meet you where you are.

Protect Your Nervous System

Stress is inevitable. What matters is how quickly your body can come back to safety. This is the heart of nervous system resilience.

Daily practices to stay regulated

- Start and end your day with one calming ritual
- Keep screens, noise, and social stimulation in check
- Use breathwork during moments of overwhelm
- Take breaks before you feel burnt out
- Say no more often and without apology

You do not need to live in stillness. You need moments of pause within your day. These moments teach your brain that rest is safe and accessible.

Expect Life to Disrupt You

A cortisol-friendly lifestyle does not mean you'll never be stressed again. Life will challenge your rhythm. You will travel. You will get sick. You will have hard weeks. None of this means you are broken or behind.

Your job is not to avoid stress. Your job is to return to balance when stress passes. Use your reset tools to ground yourself. Drink a nourishing meal. Take a slow walk. Say no when needed. Breathe deeply. Sleep early.

Every time you come back to rhythm, you strengthen your resilience.

Define Your Personal Maintenance Plan

Before you end this chapter, write down your core support plan. Include the habits, foods, movement, and rituals that make you feel most balanced. Think of this as your return-to-rhythm list.

Examples may include:

- Morning sunlight and protein-rich breakfast
- Midday walk and magnesium-rich lunch
- No caffeine after noon
- Screen-free evening with herbal tea
- Sunday evening planning and reset time

This plan is yours. Keep it flexible, honest, and doable. Revisit it every month and adjust based on your life season.

You are not starting over. You are continuing forward with wisdom and rhythm. This is not the end of your reset. This is the beginning of a lifestyle that supports the healthiest version of you for life.

PART IV: DETOX-FRIENDLY RECIPES FOR HORMONE BALANCE & FAT BURN

Sleep-Supporting Meals

The first meal of your day plays a powerful role in regulating cortisol. When you eat a blood sugar-stabilizing, protein-rich breakfast within **60** minutes of waking, you prevent a cortisol spike and set the tone for calm, focused energy. Skipping breakfast or grabbing sugary, carb-heavy foods sends your body into stress mode and kicks off a chain reaction of cravings, irritability, and afternoon crashes.

These ten cortisol-conscious breakfasts are quick to make, easy to digest, and designed to balance hormones, fuel your morning, and curb belly fat storage.

1. Savory Veggie Omelet with Avocado

Whisk two eggs and cook with olive oil, chopped spinach, and red bell pepper. Serve with half an avocado and a sprinkle of sea salt.

Why it works: Packed with protein, healthy fats, and anti-inflammatory nutrients that slow digestion and support adrenal recovery.

2. Greek Yogurt Bowl with Chia and Berries

Combine ¾ cup full-fat plain Greek yogurt with **1** tablespoon chia seeds, ¼ cup blueberries, and a handful of walnuts. Drizzle with cinnamon and a touch of raw honey if desired.

Why it works: Rich in probiotics, fat, and fiber. Supports gut health, stabilizes blood sugar, and satisfies sweet cravings without the crash.

3. Sweet Potato Breakfast Hash

Sauté chopped sweet potato, kale, and turkey sausage in coconut oil. Top with a fried egg.

Why it works: Complex carbs + protein + fat = cortisol-friendly. This combo reduces inflammation and keeps you full for hours.

4. Almond Butter Chia Oats

Soak ½ cup rolled oats overnight in almond milk with **1** tablespoon chia seeds. In the morning, stir in a tablespoon of almond butter and top with sliced banana.

Why it works: Provides slow-release carbs, fiber, and fat to help avoid blood sugar crashes and mid-morning anxiety.

5. Coconut Flour Pancakes with Turkey Bacon

Make a quick pancake with coconut flour, eggs, and almond milk. Serve with **2** strips of nitrate-free turkey bacon and a side of sliced apple.

Why it works: Low in sugar and high in protein and fat. A delicious way to satisfy morning hunger without spiking insulin.

6. Avocado Toast on Sprouted Bread with Egg

Toast one slice of sprouted grain bread, top with mashed avocado, sea salt, and a poached or fried egg. Add red pepper flakes for flavor.

Why it works: Balanced in fat, carbs, and protein. Keeps cortisol stable and fuels your brain for a focused morning.

7. Tofu Scramble with Mushrooms and Greens

Crumble firm tofu in a skillet and cook with olive oil, garlic, mushrooms, and spinach. Add turmeric for extra anti-inflammatory power.

Why it works: Plant-based protein, iron, and antioxidants. Supports hormone balance without overwhelming your system.

8. Protein Smoothie with Greens and Berries

Blend **1** scoop clean protein powder, ½ banana, **1** tablespoon flaxseed, spinach, and unsweetened almond milk.

Why it works: A quick, portable option that hits all your macronutrient needs and cools inflammation.

9. Egg Muffins with Veggies and Goat Cheese

Whisk **4–6** eggs, pour into muffin tins, and add chopped veggies like zucchini, tomato, and kale. Sprinkle goat cheese on top and bake at **350**°F for **20** minutes.

Why it works: Easy to prep in advance. Rich in protein, calcium, and micronutrients that support adrenal repair.

10. Quinoa Breakfast Bowl with Pumpkin Seeds and Apple

Warm up ½ cup cooked quinoa and top with diced apple, pumpkin seeds, a drizzle of almond milk, and cinnamon.

Why it works: Grain-based but balanced with protein and fat. The fiber and minerals help stabilize blood sugar and promote calm.

More Hormone-Balancing Breakfasts to Lower Cortisol

(**10** more recipes, **800** words)

A cortisol-conscious morning routine begins with food that calms, not triggers. Every breakfast is a chance to reset your hormones and metabolism before the day demands your energy. These ten additional breakfast recipes are rich in nutrients, low in sugar, and crafted to keep cortisol steady while promoting fat loss, satiety, and stress resilience.

11. Smoked Salmon and Cucumber Wraps

Spread cream cheese on two large romaine lettuce leaves. Add smoked salmon slices, cucumber sticks, and a sprinkle of dill or capers. Roll and enjoy.

Why it works: High in protein and omega-**3** fats, this no-carb breakfast reduces inflammation and supports brain function.

12. Cottage Cheese Bowl with Pear and Walnuts

Scoop ¾ cup full-fat cottage cheese into a bowl. Top with sliced pear, walnuts, and cinnamon. Add ground flaxseed for extra fiber.

Why it works: Combines protein, fat, and fiber to stabilize insulin and reduce the post-breakfast energy crash.

13. Ground Turkey and Zucchini Skillet

Brown ½ cup ground turkey with chopped zucchini, garlic, and onion. Add a spoonful of salsa or avocado on top.

Why it works: A savory, blood sugar-stabilizing option rich in protein and potassium to start your day strong.

14. Protein-Packed Chia Pudding

Soak **3** tablespoons chia seeds in almond milk overnight. In the morning, stir in collagen peptides or protein powder, then top with sliced almonds and blueberries.

Why it works: High in healthy fats, protein, and fiber. Supports digestive health, satiety, and calm energy.

15. Breakfast Burrito Bowl

In a bowl, layer scrambled eggs, sautéed spinach, black beans, and avocado. Top with a little salsa or nutritional yeast.

Why it works: This hormone-balancing bowl offers a perfect combination of healthy fats, fiber, and slow-burning carbs.

16. Stuffed Avocado with Tuna or Egg Salad

Halve an avocado and fill the center with a scoop of tuna salad (tuna, olive oil, celery) or egg salad (boiled eggs, mustard, Greek yogurt).

Why it works: This no-cook breakfast is rich in B vitamins and healthy fats to lower inflammation and support adrenal health.

17. Lentil and Sweet Potato Breakfast Bowl

Warm cooked lentils and cubed sweet potatoes in a pan with coconut oil and season with turmeric and cumin. Serve with a dollop of plain Greek yogurt.

Why it works: Fiber-rich lentils and complex carbs from sweet potatoes help with sustained energy and better hormone function.

18. Almond Flour Banana Muffins (Prep Ahead)

Bake muffins with almond flour, mashed banana, eggs, and cinnamon. Use a touch of maple syrup if desired and freeze for easy grab-and-go mornings.

Why it works: Grain-free but satisfying, these muffins deliver protein and fat without spiking your blood sugar.

19. Mini Chicken Sausage Patties with Apple Slices

Form ground chicken into small patties seasoned with sage, salt, and garlic. Cook in a pan and serve with sliced apple and almond butter.

Why it works: A hearty, protein-rich meal that balances sweet and savory, keeping cortisol low and energy stable.

20. Buckwheat Porridge with Hemp Seeds and Coconut

Simmer ½ cup buckwheat groats in coconut milk until soft. Stir in hemp seeds, cinnamon, and a spoon of sunflower butter.

Why it works: Gluten-free and high in magnesium and plant-based protein. A great option for calming the nervous system.

Breakfast Reminders for Cortisol Balance

- Make it savory more often than sweet. Sweet breakfasts can spike cortisol and insulin. A savory meal helps you stay grounded and focused.
- Use herbs and spices. Cinnamon, turmeric, and cumin not only enhance flavor but support blood sugar control and inflammation reduction.
- Prep in advance. Keep egg muffins, turkey patties, or chia pudding ready to grab. Less decision fatigue in the morning reduces stress.
- Pair carbs with protein and fat. Never eat a carb on its own. That includes fruit, toast, or oats. Always balance your plate.
- Eat within **60** minutes of waking to prevent a cortisol spike.
- Aim for at least **20** grams of protein at breakfast. This supports hormone production and keeps cravings at bay.

Bloat-Free Lunches

Lunch is the bridge between your morning energy and your evening wind-down. It plays a key role in whether you stay calm and focused or crash and crave sugar by mid-afternoon. A well-balanced lunch stabilizes blood sugar, supports cortisol balance, and keeps insulin from spiking—reducing belly fat, brain fog, and irritability.

These **10** recipes are quick to assemble, nutrient-dense, and specifically designed to help women in cortisol recovery avoid the slump and support sustainable energy without relying on caffeine or snacks.

1. Grilled Chicken Salad with Olive Oil and Avocado

Top mixed greens with grilled chicken breast, avocado slices, cherry tomatoes, cucumber, and a handful of sunflower seeds. Dress with olive oil and lemon juice.

Why it works: Protein and healthy fats keep blood sugar stable. Fiber from greens and seeds slows digestion and promotes satiety.

2. Tuna and Chickpea Bowl

Mix canned tuna in olive oil with chickpeas, chopped parsley, cucumber, and red onion. Drizzle with tahini and lemon.

Why it works: A protein-fiber combo that keeps cravings away and fuels your brain. Chickpeas add resistant starch for gut support.

3. Zucchini Noodles with Pesto and Grilled Shrimp

Sauté spiralized zucchini in olive oil, then toss with grilled shrimp and a spoonful of homemade basil pesto.

Why it works: Low in carbs but high in nutrients and flavor. Shrimp provides lean protein and zinc, supporting thyroid and cortisol regulation.

4. Turkey Lettuce Wraps with Hummus

Spread hummus inside large romaine or butter lettuce leaves. Add sliced turkey breast, shredded carrots, and avocado slices. Wrap and eat with a side of olives.

Why it works: This light but satisfying lunch is easy on digestion and rich in cortisol-calming fats.

5. Salmon and Sweet Potato Bowl

Top cooked sweet potato cubes with flaked cooked salmon, sautéed kale, and a dollop of plain Greek yogurt. Season with garlic and lemon.

Why it works: Sweet potatoes support hormone function, while salmon delivers omega-**3**s to lower inflammation.

6. Quinoa Tabouli with Chicken and Feta

Cook quinoa and cool slightly. Mix with chopped parsley, mint, cucumber, and tomatoes. Add grilled chicken strips and crumbled feta.

Why it works: This Mediterranean-inspired bowl balances protein and complex carbs. Mint and parsley support digestion and liver detox pathways.

7. Stuffed Bell Peppers with Ground Turkey

Roast halved bell peppers and fill them with ground turkey sautéed with onions, garlic, spinach, and a few black beans. Top with nutritional yeast or shredded cheese.

Why it works: High in protein, iron, and fiber. Great for batch cooking and reheating during busy workdays.

8. Asian Chicken and Broccoli Stir-Fry

Sauté chicken breast in coconut oil with garlic, broccoli, snap peas, and shredded carrots. Splash with coconut aminos and top with sesame seeds.

Why it works: A fast, one-pan meal that provides complete nutrition without processed sauces or added sugar.

9. Lentil and Arugula Power Bowl

Combine cooked lentils with baby arugula, roasted beets, goat cheese, walnuts, and balsamic vinaigrette.

Why it works: Lentils are rich in folate and slow-digesting carbs. The variety of textures and flavors keeps this plant-based meal satisfying and blood sugar stable.

10. Egg and Veggie Scramble Bowl

Whisk two eggs and scramble with mushrooms, zucchini, bell peppers, and spinach. Serve over cooked brown rice or cauliflower rice and top with avocado slices.

Why it works: This breakfast-for-lunch option keeps things simple. Eggs deliver choline and protein, while vegetables and fiber keep cortisol in check.

Blood Sugar-Stabilizing Lunches for All-Day Energy

11. Egg Salad over Arugula and Quinoa

Mash hard-boiled eggs with olive oil, mustard, and chopped celery. Serve over a bed of arugula and a scoop of cooked quinoa. Add sliced cucumbers or radishes for crunch.

Why it works: The combination of protein, fat, and slow carbs supports blood sugar while offering steady, satisfying energy.

12. Grilled Chicken Collard Wraps

Use collard greens as a wrap and fill them with grilled chicken, avocado, shredded carrots, and tahini. Serve with a side of sauerkraut or pickles.

Why it works: Low-carb and anti-inflammatory, this lunch supports digestion and keeps cortisol levels steady.

13. Turkey and Veggie Meatballs with Cauliflower Rice

Bake ground turkey meatballs mixed with zucchini, garlic, and oregano. Serve over warm cauliflower rice with a drizzle of olive oil.

Why it works: High protein and fiber, low carb, and rich in minerals that support hormonal balance.

14. Bison Burger Lettuce Wraps

Grill a grass-fed bison patty and serve in a lettuce wrap with grilled onions, tomato, and avocado. Add a side of roasted sweet potato cubes.

Why it works: Bison offers lean protein and iron. The fat and fiber from avocado and sweet potato prevent blood sugar spikes.

15. Roasted Veggie Bowl with Poached Egg

Roast Brussels sprouts, carrots, and red onion in olive oil. Top with a poached egg and pumpkin seeds. Add a dollop of plain yogurt if desired.

Why it works: Rich in antioxidants, fiber, and hormone-supportive nutrients. The egg adds complete protein to stabilize appetite.

16. Canned Salmon Salad with Olive Tapenade

Mix canned salmon with chopped olives, parsley, and a squeeze of lemon. Serve with a handful of baby spinach and a slice of seeded gluten-free toast.

Why it works: Omega-**3** fats from salmon reduce inflammation, while olives provide healthy fats to support stress resilience.

17. Stuffed Acorn Squash with Chicken and Spinach

Roast halved acorn squash. Fill with cooked ground chicken sautéed with spinach and garlic. Top with a sprinkle of hemp seeds.

Why it works: Slow-digesting carbs, fiber, and protein keep insulin levels balanced and energy steady.

18. Thai-Inspired Chicken Salad

Toss shredded chicken with shredded cabbage, sliced bell peppers, chopped peanuts, and a dressing made of lime juice and almond butter.

Why it works: Crunchy and colorful, this lunch balances blood sugar while providing vitamin C and healthy fats to reduce stress markers.

19. Tempeh Stir-Fry with Bok Choy and Brown Rice

Sauté sliced tempeh with bok choy, carrots, and snap peas. Season with ginger, garlic, and coconut aminos. Serve over brown rice.

Why it works: A plant-based option rich in fermented protein, fiber, and anti-inflammatory spices to support cortisol control.

20. Chicken and Avocado Power Bowl

Layer spinach, shredded cabbage, grilled chicken, sliced avocado, roasted red peppers, and sunflower seeds. Drizzle with tahini dressing.

Why it works: A colorful, protein-rich bowl with anti-inflammatory fats and minerals that help regulate blood sugar and reduce fatigue.

These lunches support your hormonal healing by stabilizing blood sugar, calming cortisol, and providing nutrients that allow your body to function without needing caffeine or snacks. Every meal is a message to your hormones, and these meals say, you are nourished, you are supported, and you are safe.

Lunchtime Strategies for Cortisol Support:

- Avoid "light" lunches made up of crackers, fruit, or only a salad. Always include a complete protein, a healthy fat, and a slow carb or fiber source.
- Use leftovers intentionally. Cook extra protein or roasted vegetables at dinner to save time during the week.
- Do not eat at your desk if you can help it. Sit down, breathe, and chew slowly. Stressful eating increases cortisol even when the food is healthy.
- Stay hydrated. Pair lunch with a glass of water infused with cucumber or lemon to support digestion and energy.

Lunch is your mid-day opportunity to reinforce safety and satiety. These meals are not just about filling your stomach. They are about communicating to your body that there is no emergency, no restriction, and no need to store fat or release stress hormones. Balanced food equals balanced energy. And balanced energy keeps your reset moving forward.

Fat-Burning Dinners

1. Lemon Herb Baked Salmon with Asparagus

Bake salmon fillets with olive oil, lemon juice, garlic, and chopped dill. Serve with steamed asparagus and a small serving of wild rice.

Why it works: Omega-**3** fats from salmon reduce inflammation, while asparagus supports detox and digestion.

2. Zucchini Noodles with Turkey Meatballs

Make turkey meatballs using ground turkey, parsley, and garlic. Serve over zucchini noodles sautéed in olive oil with tomato sauce.

Why it works: Low in carbs, high in protein, and packed with anti-inflammatory herbs and vegetables.

3. Grilled Chicken with Cauliflower Mash and Broccoli

Grill or bake seasoned chicken breasts. Serve with mashed cauliflower made with garlic and ghee and steamed broccoli on the side.

Why it works: This meal provides lean protein, cruciferous vegetables, and healthy fats to lower cortisol and promote fat loss.

4. Coconut Curry Shrimp with Spinach

Sauté shrimp in coconut oil, garlic, turmeric, and curry powder. Add baby spinach and simmer with coconut milk until cooked. Serve with cauliflower rice.

Why it works: Anti-inflammatory spices, healthy fat from coconut, and protein help repair tissues and reduce belly fat.

5. Stuffed Bell Peppers with Quinoa and Ground Bison

Roast halved bell peppers filled with ground bison, cooked quinoa, onions, and chopped spinach. Season with cumin and smoked paprika.

Why it works: Bison is rich in iron and zinc, while quinoa and vegetables provide slow-burning carbs and fiber.

6. Ginger Garlic Chicken Stir-Fry with Bok Choy

Stir-fry chicken breast slices with bok choy, carrots, and snow peas in sesame oil with fresh ginger and garlic. Serve with a small portion of brown rice.

Why it works: Balanced and light, this stir-fry supports digestion and provides steady energy without triggering inflammation.

7. Roasted Vegetable Bowl with Soft-Boiled Eggs

Roast a mix of Brussels sprouts, carrots, and red onion in olive oil and rosemary. Serve with two soft-boiled eggs and a drizzle of tahini.

Why it works: This plant-based option offers healthy fats, fiber, and antioxidants to reduce inflammation and regulate hormones.

8. Sautéed Cod with Sweet Potato and Kale

Cook cod fillets with lemon, olive oil, and fresh thyme. Serve with roasted sweet potato cubes and wilted kale.

Why it works: Cod is light and easy to digest, while sweet potatoes help regulate insulin and reduce cravings.

9. Beef and Cabbage Stir-Fry with Avocado

Brown lean ground beef with garlic, ginger, and shredded cabbage. Serve with sliced avocado and a sprinkle of sesame seeds.

Why it works: High in protein and monounsaturated fats, this meal reduces inflammation and supports hormone balance.

10. Eggplant and Lentil Stew with Fresh Basil

Simmer chopped eggplant, lentils, tomatoes, onion, and garlic in olive oil and herbs. Top with fresh basil before serving.

Why it works: A fiber-rich, plant-based dinner that supports gut health and reduces bloating and cortisol levels.

11. Herb-Rubbed Grilled Chicken with Roasted Carrots and Beets

Marinate chicken breasts in olive oil, garlic, thyme, and oregano. Grill and serve with roasted carrots and beets drizzled with balsamic vinegar.

Why it works: Colorful root vegetables reduce inflammation and support liver detox while grilled herbs provide antioxidant benefits.

12. Wild-Caught Cod with Quinoa and Sautéed Spinach

Bake cod fillets with olive oil, lemon zest, and parsley. Serve with a scoop of quinoa and lightly sautéed spinach with garlic.

Why it works: Lean protein with greens and a gluten-free grain helps reduce bloat and supports hormonal fat loss.

13. Cabbage and Mushroom Stir-Fry with Tofu

Sauté shredded green cabbage and sliced mushrooms in coconut oil. Add tofu cubes and season with tamari, ginger, and garlic.

Why it works: Plant-based and fiber-rich, this stir-fry supports digestion and reduces inflammation in estrogen-sensitive pathways.

14. Roasted Butternut Squash and Turkey Sausage Bowl

Roast butternut squash cubes and serve with sliced turkey sausage and a side of sautéed kale. Sprinkle with hemp seeds.

Why it works: This comforting bowl supports blood sugar control and provides protein without heaviness.

15. Chicken Zoodle Soup with Turmeric and Lemon

Simmer chicken breast, zucchini noodles, carrots, celery, turmeric, and lemon juice in bone broth. Garnish with parsley.

Why it works: Bone broth supports gut lining repair while turmeric reduces systemic inflammation.

16. Lamb and Cauliflower Mash with Garlic Green Beans

Grill or pan-sear lamb chops with rosemary and garlic. Serve with mashed cauliflower and steamed green beans sautéed in ghee.

Why it works: Lamb is rich in zinc and healthy fats, while green vegetables support hormone detoxification.

17. Stuffed Portobello Mushrooms with Lentils and Herbs

Fill large roasted portobello caps with a mixture of cooked lentils, diced tomatoes, onions, and Italian herbs. Bake and serve with arugula.

Why it works: A vegetarian option high in fiber, iron, and anti-inflammatory phytonutrients.

18. Eggplant and Ground Turkey Skillet with Basil

Sauté cubed eggplant with ground turkey, tomatoes, onion, and garlic in olive oil. Add fresh basil at the end and serve warm.

Why it works: A low-carb, nutrient-rich skillet that balances blood sugar and reduces cravings.

19. Shrimp and Avocado Lettuce Wraps

Fill butter lettuce leaves with grilled shrimp, avocado slices, shredded cabbage, and a light lime dressing. Serve with a side of sliced cucumber.

Why it works: High in protein and healthy fats, this meal supports insulin sensitivity and reduces post-meal inflammation.

20. Beef and Sweet Potato Hash with Red Peppers

Cook ground grass-fed beef with diced sweet potatoes, red bell peppers, and spinach. Season with cumin, paprika, and black pepper.

Why it works: A grounding, anti-inflammatory option rich in vitamin C and B vitamins to support adrenal function.

Craving Crushers

1. Almond Butter and Apple Slices

Slice one small apple and pair with one tablespoon of almond butter. Sprinkle cinnamon on top for extra blood sugar support.

Why it works: This classic pairing offers fiber, fat, and a hint of natural sweetness to satisfy hunger without causing a sugar crash.

2. Hard-Boiled Eggs with Sea Salt and Paprika

Peel two hard-boiled eggs, slice in half, and sprinkle with sea salt and paprika or turmeric.

Why it works: Rich in protein and healthy fats, eggs curb cravings while providing choline to support hormone production.

3. Chia Pudding with Coconut Milk and Berries

Mix three tablespoons of chia seeds with half a cup of coconut milk. Let sit until thickened and top with fresh berries.

Why it works: A fiber-rich, hormone-friendly snack that keeps you full and supports steady blood sugar levels.

4. Avocado Rice Cakes with Hemp Seeds

Spread mashed avocado on two brown rice cakes and sprinkle with hemp seeds and a pinch of sea salt.

Why it works: A satisfying combination of complex carbs, fat, and protein that calms cortisol and reduces sugar cravings.

5. Cucumber Slices with Hummus

Slice cucumber into rounds and serve with three tablespoons of hummus. Add a dash of smoked paprika or olive oil for flavor.

Why it works: This cooling snack hydrates, nourishes, and delivers a balance of plant-based fat and protein.

6. Greek Yogurt with Pumpkin Seeds and Cinnamon

Top plain full-fat Greek yogurt with one tablespoon pumpkin seeds and a dusting of cinnamon. Add a few blueberries if desired.

Why it works: This combo supports digestion, balances hormones, and satisfies the need for something creamy and filling.

7. Turkey Roll-Ups with Dijon Mustard

Roll nitrate-free turkey slices with a thin layer of Dijon mustard and a strip of cucumber or avocado. Secure with a toothpick if needed.

Why it works: A protein-dense, low-carb snack that keeps you full and avoids blood sugar swings.

8. Frozen Banana Slices with Nut Butter Drizzle

Slice a banana, freeze the pieces, and drizzle with almond or peanut butter before serving. Optional sprinkle of cacao nibs.

Why it works: A cold, sweet treat with enough fat and fiber to curb dessert cravings without refined sugar.

9. Olives and Baby Carrots

Pair five to six olives with a handful of baby carrots for a savory, crunchy combination.

Why it works: Healthy fats from olives paired with crunchy vegetables make this a simple, satisfying snack that supports hormone balance.

10. Protein Smoothie Bites

Blend one scoop of protein powder with a little almond milk, oats, and sunflower seed butter. Scoop into small balls and chill.

Why it works: These bite-sized snacks are easy to prep and packed with protein and healthy fats to satisfy hunger between meals.

11. Roasted Chickpeas with Garlic and Paprika

Toss canned chickpeas with olive oil, garlic powder, and paprika. Roast at **400**°F until crispy.

Why it works: High in fiber and plant protein, roasted chickpeas satisfy crunch cravings and help regulate blood sugar.

12. Coconut Energy Balls with Dates and Seeds

Blend dates, shredded coconut, flaxseed, chia seeds, and a touch of nut butter. Form into small balls and refrigerate.

Why it works: These no-bake bites provide a balanced mix of natural sugars, fiber, and fat to ease sweet cravings.

13. Celery Sticks with Cashew Cream Cheese

Fill celery sticks with a dollop of cashew-based cream cheese and top with cracked black pepper or crushed walnuts.

Why it works: Crunchy and creamy, this snack delivers texture and fat to calm the nervous system and curb stress eating.

14. Edamame with Sea Salt and Sesame Oil

Steam shelled edamame and toss with a drizzle of sesame oil and a pinch of sea salt.

Why it works: Rich in plant-based protein and magnesium, this snack supports hormonal calm and helps reduce carb cravings.

15. Dark Chocolate Square with Almonds

Pair one to two squares of **85** percent dark chocolate with a handful of raw almonds.

Why it works: Dark chocolate contains magnesium and mood-boosting compounds. The fat and fiber from almonds balance its effects on blood sugar.

16. Carrot and Zucchini Muffins with Almond Flour

Bake muffins using almond flour, grated carrots and zucchini, eggs, and cinnamon. Keep them unsweetened or lightly sweetened with applesauce.

Why it works: Fiber-rich and gluten-free, these muffins satisfy the need for baked goods without triggering cravings.

17. Boiled Beet Slices with Balsamic and Walnuts

Slice cooked beets and drizzle with balsamic vinegar. Sprinkle chopped walnuts on top.

Why it works: Beets support liver detox and blood flow. Paired with walnuts, they offer texture and nutrients to reduce afternoon fatigue.

18. Canned Sardines with Cucumber and Lemon

Place sardines on cucumber rounds and top with a squeeze of lemon. Optionally add cracked pepper.

Why it works: Sardines are rich in omega-**3** fats and protein, helping to stabilize mood and hunger while reducing inflammation.

19. Pear Slices with Tahini

Slice a ripe pear and drizzle with tahini. Sprinkle a little cinnamon or sesame seeds on top.

Why it works: The natural sweetness of pear paired with healthy fat and a touch of spice helps reduce the urge for sugary desserts.

20. Avocado Chocolate Mousse

Blend ripe avocado with unsweetened cocoa powder, a splash of almond milk, and a small amount of honey or stevia. Chill before serving.

Why it works: A creamy, satisfying treat that offers healthy fat, magnesium, and a dessert-like texture without processed sugar.

Smart Dinner Strategies for Lowering Inflammation and Belly Fat

1. Include cruciferous vegetables three to four times per week

Add broccoli, Brussels sprouts, cabbage, or kale to dinner. These vegetables help detox excess estrogen and support liver function, reducing hormonal belly fat and inflammation.

2. Cook with anti-inflammatory spices

Use turmeric, ginger, cumin, and garlic in your meals. These spices reduce systemic inflammation and enhance digestion without adding calories or stress to your body.

3. Eat at least two hours before bedtime

Allow your body time to digest before sleep. Late-night eating disrupts melatonin production and keeps cortisol elevated, which can interfere with fat loss and sleep quality.

4. Prioritize protein and fiber over starch at night

Base dinners around lean protein and vegetables, with moderate slow carbs if needed. This keeps insulin and blood sugar stable overnight and improves fat metabolism.

Cortisol-Calming Drinks

1. Chamomile Lavender Tea

Steep one chamomile tea bag with a few dried lavender buds in hot water for five to seven minutes.

Why it works: Chamomile supports nervous system relaxation while lavender calms anxiety and promotes deep sleep.

2. Holy Basil (Tulsi) Tea

Brew a cup of dried tulsi leaves or use a tea bag in hot water for five minutes.

Why it works: Holy basil is a powerful adaptogen that lowers stress hormones and reduces inflammation.

3. Lemon Balm and Mint Tea

Combine equal parts lemon balm and peppermint leaves, steep for five to seven minutes, and serve warm.

Why it works: Lemon balm soothes the nervous system and peppermint eases digestion, both of which help lower cortisol.

4. Ashwagandha Golden Milk

In a small pot, warm almond milk with half a teaspoon each of ashwagandha powder, turmeric, cinnamon, and a pinch of black pepper. Whisk and sweeten with honey if desired.

Why it works: Ashwagandha helps regulate cortisol, and turmeric reduces systemic inflammation, making this a bedtime favorite.

5. Licorice Root and Ginger Tea

Steep sliced licorice root and fresh ginger in boiling water for seven to ten minutes. Strain and sip slowly.

Why it works: Licorice supports adrenal recovery and ginger aids digestion. This combination works well during afternoon fatigue.

6. Reishi Mushroom Cacao Elixir

Blend one cup of hot almond milk with one teaspoon reishi mushroom powder, one tablespoon raw cacao, cinnamon, and a touch of maple syrup.

Why it works: Reishi promotes deep relaxation and cacao contains magnesium, making it ideal for reducing stress cravings.

7. Fennel and Cardamom Digestive Tea

Crush one teaspoon of fennel seeds and a few cardamom pods. Steep in hot water for five to ten minutes and strain.

Why it works: These warming herbs reduce bloat, calm the gut, and ease nervous tension linked to cortisol spikes.

8. Cinnamon Vanilla Rooibos Tea

Steep rooibos tea with a cinnamon stick and a splash of vanilla extract. Serve hot or chilled.

Why it works: Rooibos is caffeine-free and rich in antioxidants. Cinnamon stabilizes blood sugar and supports hormonal balance.

9. Peppermint and Nettle Infusion

Mix dried peppermint and nettle leaves, steep in hot water for six to eight minutes, and strain before drinking.

Why it works: Nettle is rich in minerals that support adrenal health and peppermint offers mental clarity without overstimulation.

10. Warm Lemon and Sea Salt Morning Drink

Combine warm water with fresh lemon juice and a pinch of sea salt. Drink first thing in the morning on an empty stomach.

Why it works: Hydrates the body, supports adrenal function, and restores minerals depleted by chronic stress. This drink also gently wakes up digestion without caffeine.

Herbal Teas and Cortisol-Calming Drinks

11. Rose and Hibiscus Tea

Steep dried rose petals and hibiscus flowers in hot water for five to seven minutes. Serve hot or over ice with a slice of lemon.

Why it works: Rose soothes emotional stress while hibiscus supports cardiovascular health and lowers blood pressure.

12. Dandelion Root Latte

Simmer roasted dandelion root in water for ten minutes, then strain and blend with warm almond milk, cinnamon, and a dash of vanilla.

Why it works: Dandelion supports liver detox and digestion, helping reduce the cortisol burden on the body.

13. Valerian Root Bedtime Tea

Steep valerian root in hot water for ten to fifteen minutes. Drink thirty minutes before bed.

Why it works: Valerian helps reduce sleep latency, quiets a racing mind, and promotes parasympathetic activation.

14. Turmeric Ginger Latte

Warm almond or coconut milk with one teaspoon turmeric, half a teaspoon ginger, cinnamon, and a pinch of black pepper. Blend and serve with a touch of honey.

Why it works: Turmeric and ginger calm inflammation and support immune function. A perfect evening alternative to sugary desserts.

15. Maca and Cinnamon Almond Milk

Blend warm almond milk with one teaspoon maca powder and half a teaspoon cinnamon. Stir and enjoy mid-morning.

Why it works: Maca supports hormonal resilience and stamina. Cinnamon helps keep blood sugar steady, reducing cortisol spikes.

16. Linden Flower and Chamomile Tea

Steep equal parts linden flowers and chamomile for five minutes. Drink after meals or before bed.

Why it works: Linden calms the heart and nervous system. Combined with chamomile, it promotes emotional and physical ease.

17. Celery Juice with Cucumber and Mint

Juice fresh celery with cucumber and mint leaves. Drink chilled in the morning.

Why it works: Hydrating and rich in minerals, this drink supports adrenal recovery and lowers inflammation.

18. Passionflower Tea

Steep dried passionflower leaves in hot water for seven minutes. Drink in the evening or during emotional overwhelm.

Why it works: Passionflower increases GABA activity in the brain, helping ease anxiety and mental overactivation.

19. Spiced Golden Rooibos

Steep rooibos with turmeric, cinnamon, and ginger. Add coconut milk and a few cloves for a warming blend.

Why it works: This caffeine-free alternative supports digestion, reduces inflammation, and keeps cortisol balanced.

20. Cucumber Mint Electrolyte Water

Infuse water with cucumber slices, mint leaves, a squeeze of lime, and a pinch of sea salt. Drink throughout the afternoon.

Why it works: Replenishes minerals lost through stress and supports hydration, one of the simplest cortisol regulators.

Tips and Tricks for Cortisol-Calming Beverages

1. Avoid sweeteners unless necessary. Natural sweeteners like raw honey or maple syrup are fine in small amounts, but sugar spikes insulin and cortisol. Keep drinks lightly sweet or unsweetened.

2. Make it a ritual. Drinking these teas and tonics slowly, without distractions, enhances their calming effect. Sip mindfully and pair with stillness or a short breathing session.

3. Time your drinks for impact. Choose energizing drinks like maca or celery juice in the morning. Use calming herbs like valerian, chamomile, or passionflower in the evening to support your natural cortisol curve.

Tips to Snack Smarter

1. Pair sweet snacks with fat or protein

If you're having fruit, add nut butter or Greek yogurt. Pairing natural sugars with fat or protein prevents spikes in blood sugar and keeps cravings from spiraling.

2. Keep prepped snacks visible and accessible

Cut veggies, make chia pudding, or prep energy balls in advance. When nourishing snacks are easy to grab, you are less likely to reach for processed options.

3. Use crunch and texture to satisfy cravings

Cravings for chips or cookies often come from a desire for crunch. Try roasted chickpeas, carrots with hummus, or cucumber slices with guacamole.

4. Snack only when truly hungry

Pause before snacking to check in with your body. Drink water or herbal tea, take a few deep breaths, and ask whether you're bored, tired, or actually hungry. This helps break unconscious eating patterns.

PART V: LIFESTYLE SUPPORT & PRINTABLE DETOX TOOLS

The Busy Woman's Guide to Cortisol-Friendly Meal Prepping

Meal prepping is one of the most effective ways to keep your cortisol in check. When meals are ready and balanced, your body feels safe. You eat at regular times, avoid blood sugar crashes, reduce decision fatigue, and skip the cycle of skipping meals or grabbing processed snacks.

The challenge for most women is finding time to prep. The goal is not perfection or spending hours in the kitchen. It is about building a system that supports your hormones, even when life is full.

This guide offers real strategies and tools to make meal prep simple, flexible, and aligned with your cortisol reset.

1. Set Your Weekly Rhythm

The key to stress-free prep is having a clear but flexible routine. Choose one or two days a week where you prep meals, parts of meals, or even just ingredients.

Common Prep Days:

- Sunday afternoon or evening
- Wednesday evening as a midweek boost

Decide Your Prep Style:

Style	Description	Best For
Full meal prep	Prepping entire meals for the week	Busy workweeks, travel, families
Partial prep	Chopping, marinating, cooking staples	Flexible eaters, food variety fans
Mix and match bin	Cooking proteins, veggies, and carbs separately	Quick assembly meals

Choose the one that fits your lifestyle and adjust weekly based on your schedule.

2. Build a Cortisol-Friendly Meal Formula

Each meal you prep should include the key elements that stabilize blood sugar and support hormone balance. Use this formula when planning any breakfast, lunch, or dinner.

Cortisol-Calming Meal Formula:

Component	Examples
Protein	Chicken, eggs, salmon, lentils, turkey
Healthy Fat	Avocado, olive oil, nuts, seeds, tahini
Fiber or Slow Carb	Quinoa, sweet potatoes, greens, broccoli
Flavor & Herbs	Garlic, ginger, turmeric, basil, parsley

These ingredients lower inflammation, improve digestion, and regulate blood sugar. Balanced meals mean your cortisol does not need to do extra work.

3. Choose Recipes that Reheat and Store Well

Some foods taste better freshly made, while others are perfect for prep. Build your menu with meals that keep their texture and flavor over a few days.

Meal Prep Favorites:

- Frittatas or egg muffins
- Baked salmon or grilled chicken
- Lentil soups or veggie stews
- Roasted vegetables
- Quinoa or rice pilafs
- Chia puddings and overnight oats
- Energy balls or snack bites

Avoid meals that get soggy, overly dry, or lose their flavor quickly. Think stable, satisfying, and simple.

4. Use a "Meal Anchor" System

Instead of prepping **15** containers of identical meals, create meal anchors. These are building blocks that can be mixed and matched during the week.

Example Meal Anchor Plan:

Category	Anchor Prep Item	Usage Ideas
Protein	Grilled turkey patties	Serve with salad, wrap in lettuce, add to bowls
Carb	Roasted sweet potatoes	Add to salads, pair with eggs, use in stir-fry
Veggie	Sautéed greens with garlic	Add to omelets, bowls, or soups
Snack	Chia pudding or energy bites	Grab-and-go snack or evening treat

This method makes prep less repetitive and more adaptable. It is especially helpful if you share meals with others or need variety.

5. Keep Tools Simple and Accessible

You do not need a massive kitchen or specialty gadgets to prep well. Keep your workspace clean and tools minimal.

Meal Prep Essentials:

- Sharp knife and cutting board
- Sheet pans for roasting
- One or two large glass containers
- Mason jars for dressings or parfaits
- A basic blender or food processor

Label your containers with a piece of tape and a marker if needed. Know what is ready to go and what needs to be eaten first.

6. Prep in Phases if You are Short on Time

If you do not have a full hour or two to prep, break it into smaller sessions. You can chop in the morning, cook at night, or prep snacks during a work break.

Micro Prep Schedule Example:

Time Block	Task
Sunday Morning	Chop vegetables and marinate proteins
Sunday Night	Cook two proteins and a carb
Monday Evening	Make snack bites or chia pudding
Wednesday Night	Refresh ingredients and reheat leftovers

Meal prep does not need to be one marathon session. A few short, consistent routines can support your hormones just as well.

7. Reuse a Few Base Menus

Instead of trying new meals each week, rotate three to five weekly menus. This removes decision fatigue and streamlines grocery shopping.

Weekly Menu Rotation Example:

Week	Main Protein	Snack Focus	Dinner Theme
1	Salmon and eggs	Greek yogurt + seeds	Sheet pan meals
2	Chicken and tofu	Energy balls + berries	Stir-fry bowls
3	Turkey and lentils	Chia pudding + nuts	Stews and soups

After a month, you will have a personalized cycle that keeps prep quick and stress low.

8. Grocery and Prep Checklist

Shopping Essentials:

- Proteins: chicken, eggs, tofu, canned salmon
- Veggies: spinach, bell peppers, zucchini, broccoli
- Carbs: quinoa, brown rice, sweet potatoes
- Fats: avocado, olive oil, coconut milk
- Snacks: chia seeds, almond butter, pumpkin seeds
- Spices: turmeric, garlic, paprika, cinnamon

Quick Prep List:

- Cook **2** proteins
- Roast **2** vegetables
- Prepare **1** carb base

- Make **2** snacks or breakfast items
- Wash and chop greens

Meal prepping for cortisol balance is not about being rigid or perfect. It is about creating space in your week so that food becomes a support, not a source of stress. The more often you prep with rhythm, the easier it becomes to stay nourished, even during the busiest days.

Start with what fits today and build from there. Your hormones will thank you for every calm, grounded bite.

Work-Life Balance Hacks to Lower Daily Stress

Cortisol thrives in chaos. When your work schedule, responsibilities, and personal life clash with no room for rest, your body treats that tension like a threat. This leads to cortisol spikes, poor sleep, increased belly fat, and chronic fatigue. You do not need a perfect schedule or an empty inbox to lower your stress. You need structure, boundaries, and intentional recovery throughout your day.

These simple, real-life strategies are designed to help you calm your nervous system while staying productive, present, and nourished. Work-life balance is not a myth. It is a rhythm you create.

1. Create a Morning Buffer

Start your day gently to prevent an early cortisol surge. Avoid checking your phone or jumping into emails immediately after waking. Cortisol naturally rises in the morning, and artificial urgency exaggerates this response.

Your morning reset buffer:

Time	Action
Within **15** min	Sunlight or step outside
Within **30** min	Light stretching or breathwork
Within **45** min	Protein-rich breakfast
After **60** min	Begin checking phone or emails

A soft start to your morning gives your nervous system space to regulate before external demands take over.

2. Set Time Boundaries, Not Just Task Lists

To lower daily stress, you need to control when you engage, not just what you do. Instead of writing endless to-do lists, time block your day with intentional pauses and protected focus.

Example Time Block Flowchart:

[Focus Work Block: **9:00–11:00** AM]

|

[Break: Walk, breathwork, snack]

|

[Admin Tasks: **11:30** AM–**12:30** PM]

|

[Lunch + Unplug: **12:30–1:30** PM]

|

[Creative Work or Meetings: **1:30–3:30** PM]

|

[Recovery Break + Stretch: **3:30–4:00** PM]

|

[Final Check-In or Light Tasks: **4:00–5:00** PM]

You are not a robot. When you pair productivity with recovery, you work better and feel calmer.

3. Protect Transitions Between Roles

Many women shift between roles rapidly without pause. You go from work to family responsibilities or from parenting to evening tasks with no reset in between. This trains your body to stay in alert mode, never settling.

Try these mini-transition resets:

- Five-minute walk before leaving your workspace
- Change clothes or wash your face after work
- Listen to calming music during your commute
- Journal one sentence about what went well today

Simple rituals help your brain switch gears and tell your cortisol response to soften.

4. Simplify Decision Fatigue

Every decision you make taxes your mental energy. From meals to meetings to messages, decision fatigue increases cortisol and decreases patience. The solution is not doing less. It is making fewer repetitive choices.

Simplify your day by automating routines:

- Eat the same breakfast or lunch Monday through Friday
- Choose two work outfits for the week and rotate
- Use default time blocks for recurring tasks

- Turn off non-urgent notifications and batch message replies

By reducing choice, you reduce stress and free your focus for what matters.

5. Reclaim 20 Minutes of White Space Daily

White space is unscheduled, unproductive time that your brain uses to recover. This is not scrolling time. It is intentional stillness.

Ideas for white space:

- Lie on your back with no distractions
- Sit outside with tea or water
- Journal freely for ten minutes
- Breathe in silence or listen to calming sounds

If you feel resistance to slowing down, that is often the sign you need it most. White space restores your nervous system's capacity to cope.

6. Evening Detox from Urgency

Your body needs to wind down before bed. Evening urgency—rushing to finish chores, watching intense shows, or checking email one last time—keeps cortisol high when it should be falling.

Create a screen-free wind-down ritual:

Time	Action
7:30 PM	Dim lights and reduce stimulation
8:00 PM	Stretch, journal, or listen to soft music
8:30 PM	Herbal tea or magnesium supplement
9:00 PM	Breathwork, reading, or light meditation

This gentle transition lowers cortisol and supports deeper sleep.

7. Say "No" Without Explanation

Overcommitment is a leading cause of chronic stress in women. Saying no does not require justification. Practice short, kind refusals to protect your energy.

Use simple language:

- "That won't work for me this week"
- "I'm not available but thank you for thinking of me"
- "I need to focus on rest right now"

Clear boundaries are self-care. They teach your body that it does not need to perform to feel safe.

8. Plan Micro-Restorative Breaks Every 90 Minutes

Your brain and body function best in short focus cycles. Every **90** minutes, cortisol naturally begins to rise unless you take a pause. Schedule short breaks to restore balance and prevent burnout.

Micro-break options (**5** to **10** minutes):

- Walk around the block or office
- Step into natural light
- Drink water slowly
- Do three rounds of **4-7-8** breathing

Micro-breaks improve your clarity and protect your energy levels.

Summary Table: Daily Stress-Reduction Plan

Time of Day	Action
Morning	Sunlight, breathwork, protein breakfast
Mid-Morning	Work focus followed by walk or snack
Midday	Unplugged lunch and digestion pause
Afternoon	Light movement or stretching
Evening	Screen-free wind-down, dim lights
Anytime	White space, boundaries, or micro-breaks

Work-life balance is not a fixed destination. It is a rhythm you adjust as you move. These simple practices lower cortisol, protect your energy, and help you stay grounded even when life is full. Small shifts done consistently are more powerful than major changes done temporarily. Begin with one or two today and let them ripple outward.

Home Environment Detox: Declutter Your Space, Calm Your Mind

Your environment shapes your stress response. A cluttered, overstimulating home sends constant signals to your nervous system that you are not safe or in control. This contributes to elevated cortisol, poor sleep, decision fatigue, and even food cravings. On the other hand, a calm and organized space helps regulate your nervous system and gives your body the peace it needs to rest, recover, and heal.

A home detox is not about perfection or minimalist design. It is about making your space feel lighter, quieter, and more aligned with the calm you are building internally.

Here is how to reset your home in a way that lowers stress and supports your cortisol detox.

1. Start with the Spaces You Use Most

Focus on the rooms where you spend the most time and where clutter is most disruptive. This is usually your bedroom, kitchen, workspace, or entryway. Choose one area to begin. Do not try to do the whole house at once.

Bedroom:

Clear off nightstands, remove laundry piles, and reduce visual clutter. Keep only one or two calming items like a book, candle, or essential oil diffuser. Make your bed each morning to create an instant sense of order.

Kitchen:

Declutter countertops by removing unused appliances and organizing everyday tools. Group healthy snacks in one bin or basket. Clean out the fridge and pantry so you know what you have and can easily grab cortisol-friendly foods.

Workspace:

Limit your workspace to essentials. Tidy your desk at the end of each day. Keep calming items nearby, like a plant or a warm light. Avoid working in cluttered or chaotic areas, even for short tasks.

2. Create Calm Corners for Rest and Reset

Every home needs one small area that signals rest. It does not need to be a separate room. It could be a chair by a window, a quiet corner with a blanket, or even a bath area with soft lighting. Use this space for tea, journaling, reading, or breathing.

Elements of a calm corner:

- A comfortable seat or cushion
- Soft lighting or a candle
- A small table or tray for tea or a journal
- Natural textures like a throw blanket or woven basket

The goal is to give your body a physical location to associate with recovery and calm.

3. Remove Visual Clutter and Reduce Overstimulation

Visual clutter increases cortisol. The more your brain has to filter and process, the more taxed your nervous system becomes. Keep surfaces clear, use closed storage, and reduce harsh colors or lighting.

Quick visual detox ideas:

- Store loose papers in folders or drawers
- Keep only a few decor items per surface

- Use soft, neutral tones for linens and rugs
- Replace bright lights with warm-toned bulbs

Noise clutter matters too. Reduce background television or loud environments. Use white noise, calming playlists, or silence when possible.

4. Set a Daily Reset Ritual for Your Space

Just as you reset your body daily, your space needs maintenance too. Create a simple five to ten minute routine to tidy key areas before bed or after work. This trains your brain to expect calm and closure, not chaos.

Examples of daily reset actions:

- Fluff pillows and fold blankets in the living area
- Clear kitchen counters after dinner
- Tidy your nightstand and lay out tomorrow's clothes
- Light a candle or diffuse essential oils as a signal to wind down

Small resets build emotional security and visual relief, both of which lower cortisol.

5. Make Room for What Matters

A detoxed space is not just about what you remove. It is also about what you add with intention. Display items that bring peace or reflect your values. This might include a favorite book, a framed quote, or a calming photo.

A home that supports your healing journey is one where your body can exhale. It does not have to be perfect. It only needs to feel like a space where your nervous system can rest.

Decluttering is not only for physical organization. It is for hormonal balance, mental clarity, and emotional grounding. Every time you choose calm in your space, your cortisol responds in kind.

21-Day Cortisol Detox Daily Workbook

A Guided Companion to Help You Lose Weight, Sleep Better & Feel Like Yourself Again

This **21**-day workbook is your hands-on companion throughout the Cortisol Detox Plan. It is designed to guide you through three weeks of intentional rhythm-building, emotional awareness, and healing support, all without overwhelm or pressure. Whether you're just starting your journey or using this workbook to stay grounded day by day, you'll find space to reflect, reset, and reconnect with your body's needs.

This isn't just about filling in boxes. It's about learning to listen to your body's signals and respond with care. You'll track progress, observe patterns, and start trusting your body's ability to heal with rhythm, nourishment, and rest.

How to Use This Workbook

- Set aside **10** to **15** minutes in the morning or evening to reflect and respond.
- Be honest. No one is grading you. There are no "right" answers.
- If you miss a day, begin again. Progress is about rhythm, not perfection.
- Use weekly reflection pages to notice changes in sleep, cravings, energy, and mood.

WEEK 1: Calm the System & Create Safety

The goal this week is not to push harder but to slow down and restore calm. You're laying the foundation for everything that follows—beginning to teach your body that it's safe again. Start noticing your rhythms without judgment.

Daily Prompts:

1. What time did I wake up and go to bed?
2. Did I eat breakfast within **60** minutes of waking?
3. What calming practice did I try today (breathwork, pause, stretch)?
4. What movement did I do, if any?
5. How did I feel physically?
6. How did I feel emotionally?
7. One thing that helped me feel calm today was:
8. One thing I want to repeat tomorrow is:

End-of-Week Reflection:

- Which calming routines worked best?
- Did my sleep or digestion improve in any way?
- What parts of the day felt most supportive?
- What challenges did I notice?
- How can I stay consistent going into Week **2**?

WEEK 2: Build Nourishment & Balance Cravings

Now that your body is learning to settle, it's time to focus on nourishment. This week emphasizes balanced meals, hydration, and tracking cravings without shame. Consistency—not restriction—is your tool for healing.

Daily Prompts:

1. Did I eat three meals today, spaced every **3**–**4** hours?
2. What protein, fat, and fiber did I include?
3. Did I drink enough water or hydrating fluids?
4. What time did I feel a craving or energy dip?
5. Did I respond with food, rest, or a calming reset?
6. What was my mood like throughout the day?
7. Did I notice a difference in my sleep or energy?
8. What felt easy or supportive today?

End-of-Week Reflection:

- What meals made me feel nourished and steady?
- What eating patterns led to energy crashes or cravings?
- How did my emotional and physical energy shift this week?
- What food or hydration habit do I want to strengthen next week?

WEEK 3: Rebuild Energy & Rediscover Confidence

As rhythm returns, this week is about stepping into your power. Your job now is to support steady energy, deepen sleep quality, and reconnect with your natural motivation and joy.

Daily Prompts:

1. How did I sleep last night? (quality, duration, interruptions)
2. What did I eat before bed, and when?
3. How did I feel this morning—energized, sluggish, anxious?

4. What gave me energy today?
5. Did I move my body? What kind of movement felt good?
6. When did I feel most like myself today?
7. What thought or action helped me feel grounded?
8. What do I want to carry into tomorrow?

End-of-Week Reflection:

- How has my energy changed compared to Day **1**?
- What sleep ritual or mindset shift supported deeper rest?
- What daily actions helped me feel like myself again?
- What confidence-building habit do I want to continue beyond the **21** days?

After Your 21 Days: A Reset You Can Return To

You don't need to be perfect to keep healing. You just need a rhythm that helps your body feel safe. Use this workbook as a tool you can return to any time life feels unsteady again.

Would you like this version styled for formatting in your final manuscript (e.g. bolded prompts, page layout suggestions)?

Cortisol Detox Daily Tracker & Reflection Journal

Weekly Meal Planner and Prep Space

Use this chart to plan your meals or prep items in advance.

Day	Breakfast	Lunch	Dinner	Prep Focus
Monday				
Tuesday				
Wednesday				
Thursday				
Friday				
Saturday				
Sunday				

Weekly Mood and Energy Tracker

Track trends in your mood and energy to see how your environment, food, rest, and routines affect your stress and resilience.

Day	Morning Mood	Energy Level	Cravings	Sleep Quality	Notes
Monday					
Tuesday					
Wednesday					
Thursday					
Friday					
Saturday					
Sunday					

Affirmations and Reset Reminders

Use these phrases when you feel discouraged, tired, or tempted to give up.

- I do not have to be perfect to make progress.
- I can return to rhythm at any moment.
- I am not behind. My body is learning safety.
- One calm breath shifts everything.
- Nourishment is an act of self-respect.

Final Note

This workbook is a mirror, not a manual. You will learn the most by showing up every day and writing honestly. Your cortisol detox is not just about reducing stress or belly fat. It is about creating a life rhythm that your nervous system can trust. This is how healing becomes your new normal.

You are not starting over. You are simply returning to what has always been yours—balance, clarity, and calm. Keep this workbook as a reset tool whenever you need to reconnect. Your body already knows the way.

www.ingramcontent.com/pod-product-compliance
Lightning Source LLC
Chambersburg PA
CBHW070747050626
46230CB00022B/296

9789371238403